Ana Pat

Your Destiny is Inside You

My life is my hobby

Your Destiny is Inside You - 2020

Translation into English: Rob Pagett
& Aleksandra Oszmianska-Pagett

ISBN: 9781698908267

Imprint: Independently published

contact@mylifeismyhobby.com

TABLE OF CONTENTS

Special thanks to Dawa Steven Sherpa from Asian Trekking (Nepal).

**For my beloved children and parents
and for you**

Many people die a hundred times during their lifetime. They die of fear, longing, regret, sadness, love or despair. I have only died once; not to stop living, but rather to start living differently.

May 11, 2008

***

One day you will understand that
you are looking for what
you already have.

***

Don't intellectualize or analyze the words in this book, and don't get too attached to them. Whenever you try to interpret, intellectualize or verbalize the text, you fall into the trap set by the mind, which seeks to take control of your inner self. The mind constantly verbalizes, interprets and intellectualizes everything, thus detaching you from the essence of true understanding. It's like watching the sunset: do it in silence and you are filled with indescribably breathtaking impressions; you feel something you can't describe. Feelings cannot be put into words. As soon as you start interpreting or using words such as "what a beautiful sunset", "what a wonderful view", you kill that beautiful, unique image. Each sunset is different, completely new, it has never been the same before and never will be again. What is born new, you kill with old words. It is only in silence, in the space between the view of the sunset and verbalization, that the unique, unrepeatable beauty of existence in its entirety is born, filling up all the cells in your body. Through incessant intellectualization and verbalization, you lose the most beautiful sensations, you escape from existence. You kill the beauty growing within you of knowing the sensations that flow from existential events.

The words contained in this book are nothing more than signposts and do not point towards any religion even to the slightest extent. Try to look in the direction they indicate. You have all the wisdom within you – you were born with it. Existence cannot be understood, only felt.

It is not in the outside
world that the essence
of your trouble lies,
but in yourself.

***

Thought is energy.
Energy is vibrations.
Vibrations attract the same vibrations.
You can't fool energy.

***

EVERYTHING IS ENERGY

All the energy that exists on Earth, and all laws that govern it did not appear at the moment that human life on this planet was conceived. This energy appeared much earlier, when the Universe as a whole was created. Humankind is merely an integral part of it. About 14 billion years ago, the first matter (singularity) exploded in the Universe - the moment called the Big Bang. The beginnings of the Universe are counted from this event. To this day, nothing on Earth nor in the Universe was created from something external. All things are closely connected with each other and are created only through evolutionary transformations taking place both in the material and spiritual world.

Initially, matter existed only in the simplest form - hydrogen atoms. Hydrogen is the simplest element with the atomic number 1. This was all that the whole Universe consisted of. Atoms attracted each other, became denser and hotter, and eventually ignited to form stars. In these stars, successive nuclear reactions took place, leading to the creation of new elements. The first stars aged and exploded, releasing new elements. The whole process began once more. Each subsequent generation of stars created matter in the Universe that had not existed before, until all the elements that exist today were created. Matter was transformed by evolution from the simplest form of energetic vibration, hydrogen particles, to the most complex form - carbon particles. The Universe was now ready for its next evolutionary leap. When the Sun was formed, the clusters of matter containing all the newly formed elements, including carbon, became denser in the orbit around it. One such cluster was the Earth itself. As the Earth's crust cooled, the gases trapped in the liquid core of the planet began to rise towards the surface, thus creating steam. Great rains fell and oceans spilled out over the surface of the Earth. Water covered most of the planet, the sky was clear, and the bright sun gave the Earth light, heat and radiation. In water bodies, under the influence of radiation, carbon molecules merged into chains of amino acids. Life was created, a new link in the evolutionary chain. The first life forms, limited solely to water bodies, developed very quickly. In the Age of Fishes, animals filled the oceans. As the Earth cooled and sufficient oxygen appeared in the atmosphere, animals also appeared on land. The first fish-like amphibians emerged from the water and began using their lungs to breathe the air. Next, matter evolved again and reptiles appeared, which took over the Earth in the great age of dinosaurs. Then it was the turn of cold-blooded mammals. Each newly emerging animal species meant that life (matter) was moving to a higher level of vibration. Eventually, the development process was over, with humankind standing at its summit. Yet evolution continues within the consciousness of every human being. This is connected with their free will and their decisions. It is these that pushed and continue to push us further.

Humans are the only creatures on Earth
who can become whatever they want to be.

Those who, for various reasons, experience a blockage in the evolution ongoing within their own consciousness, their own inner world, are ruled by hedonistic pleasures delivered to their senses. Intellectual pleasures are sidelined or are absent. Undoubtedly, such people can devote hours to their external appearance, shopping or social gatherings that contribute nothing to their life. They will always enjoy spending time with their friends, laughing their heads off at a joke they've heard for the hundredth time. They love being in crowds, where there is always something going on. They feel very bad in isolation. They like to be everywhere, they are ready to do anything to just drown out the voice of their heart. Leading such a life makes it extremely difficult to pick up signals from the higher levels of consciousness. This does not mean that there are no such signals: they always exist and are everywhere, albeit sent on other frequencies that are not picked up at this level. Just because someone listens to a radio broadcast on certain frequencies does not mean that no other program is being broadcast. Such a lifestyle does not necessarily mean that at some point they will not feel the need to develop spiritually. For various reasons, they may "jam" the signal and start to receive others from higher frequencies. Most frequently it is the case that having received a signal resonating with their own hearts at least once, with the passage of time they start to receive these signals more and more frequently. Those who have received light from higher levels will never forget that another world exists, one much more valuable, much more interesting, much more joyful. In such a situation, they are no longer able to turn back from the road leading them towards this light. Someone who once entered the path of development towards the light, opened his or her heart and felt its true power, can no longer leave that path. However, we must remember that this is a very dangerous path and one only for the brave. Before you reach your destination, many of its stages must be overcome in a state of uncertainty and solitude. Some things that have gone unpunished until now, and remain in the darkness, are now immediately discerned, and the consequences of bad deeds will become all the more severe.

***

In order to better understand how long humankind has existed in the Universe or inhabited the Earth as an inseparable part of this system, let's divide the history of the Universe by 1 billion and imagine that it was created 14 years ago. The Earth was created 4.5 years ago, while humans have inhabited the Earth for about 40 minutes. Civilization as we know it now has existed for a mere 3 seconds. Looking proportionately at the history of the Universe, the

Earth and humankind on it, it is clear that we have only been here for quite literally a moment.

***

The world's most famous equation, Albert Einstein's $E=MC^2$, completely changed the Newtonian perception of the world until that point. Before Einstein's discovery, it was believed that matter and energy are two concepts with nothing in common. Through the equation $E=MC^2$, Einstein proved where energy (E) equals mass (M) multiplied by the speed of light (C) squared, and that matter is nothing but energy vibrating at a certain level. This means that what we consider matter, a solid physical body, is only a collection of tiny particles of vibrating energy at different levels, frequencies. You might say that everything around us, the whole Universe, is one great Ocean of Energy. Here, where the energy vibrates on low vibrations, tiny, invisible particles are concentrated very closely together, thus forming a solid body. The lower the vibrations, the more compressed these particles are: they form hard matter. A simplified example of this phenomenon is water. The chemical formula for water is H_2O. Water is nothing but a combination of two hydrogen (H) and one oxygen (O) molecule. These two gases, which are invisible to the naked eye, are connected together but vibrate at high frequencies are still invisible. When their vibrations decrease slightly, we see them as water vapor (H_2O). When their vibrations decrease further still, reducing the energy inside, what is invisible in the initial phase as two gases takes the form of soft matter, which we see in the form of ordinary water (H_2O). With an even greater decrease in vibrations and a decrease in internal energy, hard matter, ice (H_2O) is formed. This means that both what we see and what we do not see is energy. Whether these are objects or our thoughts, everything is energy, energy that is present throughout the Universe.

To understand this phenomenon better, let's create a small and highly simplified visualization. Imagine a very small particle, invisible to the naked eye – let's call it an elementary particle, an atom or anything else. If we add another invisible particle one by one, we will finally be able to see something. If we have a lot of time, we will ultimately produce quite a big object out of "nothing", let's say a rock. Of course, we can reverse this process. If we are lucky and we have some small pliers at hand, we can take one particle at a time out of our rock. The result of our work will be that there is no more rock and we will not see anything else. And yet nobody has stolen anything.

So now can you imagine that everything is energy?

The moment you stop being afraid of what others say, you become a free.

***

It's not reality that matters,
but how you see it and explain
it to yourself.

***

EVERYTHING IS ONE

The energies in the Universe interact with each other, creating a uniform and coherent energy system. Humankind is just an integral part of this. Whether it wants this or not, humankind is an inseparable element of this energy system and is subject to all the laws that govern it. There is no way out of the Energy System of the Universe; let us call it the Spiritual Energy of the Universe.

Everything on Earth -trees, mountains, seas, animals and the human race - is closely bound together and shares one common energy. This is the invisible but perceptible energy of the Universe, the energy which can be called life, and which religions call God. This energy is in constant motion, both in the inner cellular space and in the most remote expanses of the Universe. We are in an unbreakable bond with it, we are part of it. Unconditionally and for ever.

The Universe is one, it is in a state of perfect harmony, an infinite vastness of energy in a state of absolute and perfect balance. Like any energy, to flow, to live, it must have its opposite poles, where the sums balance themselves out at both ends of the extreme. It is a perfect, self-regulating energy system, where the number of positively charged particles equals the number of negatively charged ones. This is the same as the sum of all the positive poles of magnets on Earth being equal to the sum of all their negative poles. The amount of positive energy is equal to the amount of negative energy. It cannot be otherwise, because the ideal system of equilibrium would be upset. This state of equilibrium ensures the existence of the whole Universe, for if it were not so, it would simply disintegrate, in accordance with the laws of physics.

Your destiny depends on your thoughts.

If anyone, through their thoughts, actions or intentions, generates an additional energy field in this perfectly balanced Universe, be it positive or negative, it will upset the balance, causing an excess of one of the poles. Every such action is an unaccomplished event, disrupting the process of equilibrium. Energy produced this way must be neutralized in the life of the person who created it. It makes no difference whether it is positive or negative energy. Neutralization, i.e. receiving the energy generated, can only take place where it was generated, that is, in a particular person. It cannot take place in the life of any other person than the one who created it, otherwise it would be "extremely unfair"; after all, the Universe is a perfect system.

The energy we produce is not always immediately returned. Sometimes we have to wait for a while for this to happen, but sooner or later the energy generated has to be neutralized. There is no doubt that we will receive the same kind of energy that we have generated, never the other way around.

In order to gain a better and deeper understanding of this process, let us produce another visualization. Imagine that in order to secure the energy balance of the Universe, every human being is surrounded by an invisible balloon which accumulates all the energy he or she produces. This balloon's task is to protect the energy system of the Universe from energy disturbances produced by particular individuals. This energy has no way to escape. It makes no difference whether the energy produced is positive or negative. Whatever the type of energy, it must not disrupt the energy of the Universe, which remains in the highest state of balance. If the time of energy accumulation, and thus waiting for its neutralization, i.e. its return to the person, is very long, this person can expect either great happiness or a great tragedy to occur in their life. One way or another, the energy generated is certain to be returned.

Human beings are the only creatures in this system equipped with the free will to live and act as they see fit. Only humans have a choice. They can live according to the laws of nature, the laws of the Spiritual Energy of the Universe, respecting and accepting them, or they can choose to follow their own path against these laws, trying to adapt their life to their own needs.

Going against the tide, living against these laws requires a great deal of energy. At first, a person may not even notice that they are going against the tide in their life, they may also find such a life very interesting and exciting, but we should remember that no one has the strength to go on swimming against the tide all their life. As time goes by, living life at variance with the Spiritual Energy of the Universe will only make this energy expenditure ever greater. If such a person does not realize it in time, while they are still strong enough, and if they don't turn back at the right moment, they will simply lose all their strength and will be swept away by the stream of life completely involuntarily, without the possibility of controlling the direction. The tide of the sea of life will carry them and smash them against the rocks. Therefore, while we still have strength, it is worth considering for a moment whether our life is not in conflict with the laws of the Spiritual Energy of the Universe.

Sailing with a current flowing from deep inside your heart, you will easily achieve everything you desire in life. All you have to do is steer well and go with the current. Life will never follow you, it is you who must follow the current of life.

***

Once we realize that the omnipresent immense power of the invisible Spiritual Energy of the Universe exists, we will be able to understand that what the senses are incapable of grasping has more power than what is visible and tangible. The connection to the source of this inexhaustible energy always begins with an awareness of its existence.

***

Everything is energy, and energy comes in waves that are sometimes high tide and at other times low tide. The awareness of constant change in our life helps us maintain balance and peace of mind. This is the only way to break the habit of reacting to the sensations that appear every moment. It does not matter whether they are positive or negative. Real life brings both ups and downs.

Would mountains exist if it wasn't
for the valleys?

At the point of high tide in your life, you feel great, you feel like doing so many things, you are open, you make new friends with ease, everything is working out. You are filled with joy, you think you can move mountains, that the whole Universe is your oyster. When everything goes well, you experience a positive vibe and become euphoric.

In this state, when external circumstances change, things start to get worse, you feel negative, you immediately lose your inner harmony, often falling into a depressive state. These are the natural consequences of being attached to existing sensations, desires or aversions which clearly contradict the eternal principle of ever-changing life, in other words the "this will change, too" principle. This does not mean that when everything is going well and your experiences are positive, you should not be happy. When you are happy, be joyful, merry and celebrate this joy. In such circumstances, you should enjoy and celebrate life to the full, but don't become attached to these experiences. Treat them more like the weather that has just come, but do not identify yourself with it. Be aware that this is the weather and it will change, according to the principle "this will change, too".

When dark clouds loom on the horizon, when your energy levels slump, this approach to life will prove very helpful. At low tide, your energy level drops, it becomes harder to take decisions, you feel apathetic, everything goes wrong, you can't maintain good relations with others, you are overwhelmed by sadness, and the whole world seems gray, deprived of any color. All this is a natural process; there is nothing wrong with it, so do not try to fight it or blame yourself or others for how things are. Learn to accept them, don't try to do anything by force. Don't create any additional trouble for yourself. When sadness hits you, experience it in full. There's nothing wrong with this approach. Sit in silence, let your sadness become a moment of peace and tranquility, but do not identify yourself with it. Treat it like the weather that has just come into your life. Be aware that according to the laws of nature, the weather is subject to cyclical changes. Let your sadness be the weather that surrounds you. Then suddenly you will see that your sadness is no longer sadness. Instead, it has become a moment of calm, peace and silence. It has become beautiful in itself. When you feel sad, be sad. Take advantage of this low ebb. Let it be your time, time to relax, rest and meditate. It's the perfect time to take care of yourself, to engage in deep reflections. This is a time to sow the new seeds of your self, so don't waste it on futile internal struggles. This merely weakens you and leads to depressive moods. If you feel that everything around you is shutting down, help it to shut down. Under no circumstances should you try to fight it, otherwise you will really expend all your energy on a pointless battle. When your energy is drained, you have no chance of winning. Wait out this period in a state of deep calm, devote it all to yourself, to your reflections.

Sometimes there are situations in life that seem unbearable, when it seems that things can't get any worse. In such cases, the only light, a lantern in the darkness, can only be found in this well-founded principle: "This will also change". It is the source of strength and allows us to "go through hell" in a state of calm.

Adversity teaches wisdom,
success takes it away.

You don't always have to be cheerful, open and smiling. Just let yourself have those bad days, don't fight it, because you will only waste the rest of your energy and you won't even be able to feel the next high tide coming.

The high tide of energy will come at the best time for you, but at that point you must be rested and relaxed. Remember that the voice of your destiny is very quiet and can only be heard in your internal silence. This tide will let you harvest the seeds you sowed at the time of low tide. These are all natural processes, so accept them, do not fight nature. With time, you will experience the greatest transformation. You will reach a climax and the realization that you are becoming an observer that nothing can shake. At that point, you will begin to celebrate life in all its aspects.

Everything that happens to us in life has its source in our intentions and is even determined by our unconscious thoughts or emotions. They influence our life experiences, affecting our energy, in turn determining our future actions and life experiences. Once you are aware of your own heart's energy, of your own soul, you start to get involved in the process of consciously creating your own life, a life that follows the Spiritual Energy of the Universe, based on a profound awareness of your own inner self. A life that reflects its values that create your future life experiences. Experiences that bring us into a state of unity and peace.

Stay away from negativity and dogmatism.

Depending on what kind of inner energy we generate in the deepest layers of our subconscious, this will be the kind of energy of the Universe with which we enter into mutual vibrations. The kind of energy field that emanates around us determines the kind of people we come across in our lives. This is not a matter of chance, just as magnets are never attracted to the wrong poles. Therefore it is always necessary to remember that a thought is also energy vibrating on a certain level, and particular vibrations always attract their own kind. Therefore, it is so important to be aware of what and how we think, and to make sure that we engage in a positive internal dialogue as well. It is not a question of the kind of energy we think we are generating, but of the kind of energy lying at the core of our lives, our thoughts, intentions and actions. If at the root of our intentions or deeds there is even a hint of negative energy, which comes from thoughts marked by fear, anxiety, insecurity, lack of faith, worry, anger, desire for revenge, dissatisfaction, jealousy, hatred or greed, we will create an aura of negative energy around us, which will impact on the energy that affects our life to come. The way we present ourselves to the outside world has no influence on the fact that the energy we produce is negative. This means that we attract everything that is generated by negative energy sources. More often than not, we are unaware of the source of energy our first intention or thought comes from, which lies at the root of the whole chain of subsequent events.

***

Parable / Metaphor:

Once upon the time, in a village somewhere, no one knows when and where, a man killed a child. He was captured and brought to trial. The court sentenced him to death, but this village had a custom that the final word belonged to the victim's mother. The court asked the despairing mother whether she was satisfied with the sentence, whether she accepted it or wanted to change it.

Before she replied, an elderly, gray-haired man approached her and said:

"If you accept the judge's verdict, you will gain a sense of justice, but you will also carry the burden of suffering for the rest of your life. But if you can forgive and decide to spare his life, then you too will be free".

Instead of searching for justice, it is better to seek the energy of forgiveness.

***

The same hands that clench in a fist can also embrace in a hug. The choice is yours. You create the energy of your own life with your decisions. The reason is of no importance, because it has already occurred and it cannot be undone. All that matters are the consequences of your decisions. They will fill you with double the energy that you have generated yourself. Anger and grief form an acid that inflicts greater damage on the vessel containing it than the surface it is poured onto. To amass love inside you is happiness, to amass hatred is a disaster.

If our thoughts and deeds are rooted in love, compassion and faith in what we do and good intentions, which do not harm anybody in any way, or are not at nature's or somebody else's expense, then we connect with the positive energy of the Universe and this energy will always support us and push us forward.

It is of particular importance that our intentions come from deep inside of our heart and that they are not merely egoistic whims of our mind. If not, we block our access to the source of true power that flows from the infinite ocean of the Spiritual Energy of the Universe.

The Energy of the Universe always responds to our expectations. It doesn't matter if these expectations are positive or negative, conscious or subconscious. Our expectations are the vibrating energy field emanating from ourselves and tuning in with the Energy of the Universe that vibrates on the same level and therefore connects with them.

By expectations I don't mean automatic repetition of our desires but being aware of them. Reciting wise words that you have read in a holy book or you've heard from somebody wise and saying them with faith and the conviction that they are powerful are two completely different things. For instance, it's not a matter of asking to be happy but of being aware of happiness in your life. A person who is forever waiting for a big change in their life which will finally make them happy does nothing but simply affirm that they are indeed unhappy. As a result, this person's energy of expectations vibrates on the level of dissatisfaction. This person cannot achieve anything other than dissatisfaction, as this is the only thing that can be found on these particular vibration levels. It has to be borne in mind that the Universe responds to our energy but doesn't change it. This energy cannot be altered, because every person has their own free will. Otherwise, we would have had to be deprived of it.

If you are not happy, it is a sign that you are concentrating on what you don't have.

People who constantly think of their life as gray, useless and bland or those who can't appreciate what they have in life, because they keep dreaming about something they lack, are the kind of people who can't love and enjoy their life. They are constantly unhappy, devoid of joy and positive spirits. Their life is filled with sadness and pain. They emanate this kind of energy, which naturally attracts the same kind of energy, and day after day all these negative feelings simply get enhanced, making their life even more gray and bland. Such people carry with them all these negative seeds of their future, of every single day of their life to come. Sadness and unhappiness can't yield joy. There is no such possibility.

People who are happy and find joy in every new day, people who are not blinded by jealousy and dissatisfaction, people who are thankful for what they've got, people who learn and develop with an optimistic outlook on the future, these are the ones who cherish the seeds of joy, out of which every new moment and every new day of their life is born. Every joyful moment brings another joyful one. Each new moment is a blessing, because it is born of joy and appreciation. Such people will definitely be rewarded with a full abundance of life.

Build fewer walls and more bridges.

Our future is born out of the seeds we carry within ourselves, the seeds we plant in the soil of our subconscious. Our subconscious is like the soil in which we plant the seeds of our future. The subconscious doesn't judge what kind of seeds they are, but looks after them and creates the best kind of conditions for each plant to grow. For example, if you plant tomatoes, then it will be tomato plants that will grow and no matter how much you prey or wish for cucumbers, it won't work. If you want cucumbers, plant cucumber seeds. You reap what you sow. It couldn't be more obvious.

If you are not satisfied with what life brings, it means you have to change the way you think and be constantly aware of your thoughts, and not only when you recall them.

This is why, every day, you should think about what you desire from the bottom of your heart. Think about success, peace, abundance and joy. Keep such images in your mind, paint the picture of your life using joyful colors. This kind of constructive thinking will take root in your subconscious and will bring you happiness and abundance.

You have to be aware of your happiness, rather than asking for it or expecting it to come to you. These two issues have nothing in common. These are the two different kinds of energy. The awareness of happiness is a very positive energy. Requests for happiness, prayers, waiting and searching for it is – this is all nothing else but generating negative energy. The same rule applies to all the other aspects of life.

You can be aware of success while learning, developing and working while maintaining a deep inner conviction that you are going to be successful in life, or you can dream about success. The awareness of success will certainly allow this to materialize it, whereas dreaming about it reinforces the lack of success. The same applies to health. A person who keeps thinking about how to follow a healthy diet, a healthy lifestyle, how to take care of their body to protect it from illness or the aging process does nothing else but affirm their fear of illness or aging. All such thoughts derive from negative energy sources, from the sources of fear and worries. They are subconscious and hidden declarations of what we don't want in life. In contrast, you need to focus your thinking on what you want rather than what you don't. If you are aware of your health, if you live and eat in a conscious manner, if you don't waste time battling with the passing of time, then you certainly support yourself with the energy of health and joy of life.

Negative thinking is the worst approach and the worst strategy for coping with any difficult situation. It usually obscures the whole picture by exaggerating the scale of the problem and therefore makes it impossible to assess the situation properly and, as a result, take the best decision. According to the law of resonance, negative energy starts to attract more and more negative energy and in this way also triggers the hidden negative processes in other people around us. Any action you put negative energy into is infected with it, and as a consequence, it will bring another disaster in the future. Moreover, a negative approach stimulates the mind to create negative visions, unnecessarily exaggerating the scale of problems.

If you are unaware of the process, you are pushed even further into deeper unconsciousness and you start attracting even more negative energy. This is how a vicious circle expands, i.e. one negative thought triggers the next one. This is how we create problems for ourselves, endlessly.

Most of your problems are mere delusions that never go beyond your own thoughts. If you learn to consciously reject them and focus on the real challenge, it will turn out that the situation is not that bad. Your greatest limitation is not those real challenges but all those imaginary and exaggerated ones. Their magnitude and their persistence. They deprive you of all energy and all your joy of life. They work like a magnet that attracts negative energy, manifesting it in creating your inner hell. Before you attempt to do anything about this, try to understand that most of these problems mean absolutely nothing, or recognize them as merely the figments of your imagination. Fueled by negative energy, the mind usually creates exaggerated and non-existent problems, and creating baseless problems is its primary role. First, the mind conjures them up, blowing them out of all proportion, and only then do you try to solve them. If, on top of that, you start to engage in any internal dialogue or discussion, you will only boost the energy of these mind-created problems. They will grow to an unprecedented size.

In every difficult situation, it's best to wait a while before you embark on any course of action. Start looking at your own thoughts consciously, reject all those that are just a projection of the reality of your own making. Learn to assess each situation as if you were just an observer looking from a distance, somebody disconnected, somebody who doesn't judge or issue any verdict. Try to look at every difficult situation not as a problem but as a challenge you want to face. This kind of approach will help you to distance yourself from the situation and will certainly give you positive energy and facilitate making the most sensible decisions. Rather than creating unimaginably horrifying visions, try to recognize most of your problems as something that doesn't exist outside of your mind and, in fact, have no great significance in your life. Over time, you will find that your mind is no longer controlling you and that the constant stream of negative thoughts is starting to fade away.

A particular situation is always the way it stands. The only thing you can do is enhance it with your negative or positive attitude. A negative attitude is certain to be of no help, and instead will only cause the problem to escalate by weakening you and hindering you in taking any action. Positive thinking will help you rise to even the biggest challenge in the best possible way.

***

Just to remind all those who don't remember it, in the history of the Universe there has never been such a storm or a night after which the Sun didn't appear! Night is simply the gateway to day.

***

If you think a turbulent time lies ahead of you and/or it seems there's only darkness around, don't fight it. You will waste a lot of energy and not even notice when the sun comes up. Accept that there are difficult moments to come in your life. Take up this challenge in a conscious and detached way, but don't fight it. If you remain calm and attentive, you will certainly see some light in a short time. Light is best seen in the dark. What's more, only a good mood will help you, while a bad mood will certainly not.

Calmly waiting out a difficult period
is the only wise decision.

All our thoughts have two sources: faith or fear. They can be either positive or negative. Whilever we remain unaware of the energy source of our thoughts, we will continue to be torn between extreme emotional states. Only energy flowing from the source of faith, love and compassion can bring the feeling of lightness, satisfaction and joy of life. All thoughts, even subconscious ones, which stem from wrath, anger, regret, jealousy, fear, desire for revenge or retaliation, feelings of guilt or harm, an egoistic drive to satisfy your own needs, both material and emotional, to create one's own power and glory, derive from a negative source. All of these have an impact on our intentions, which shape their own reality. This reality is illusory, it is created by our own negative energy, it is determined by our negative, sometimes unconscious, intentions and thoughts. All this has an impact on our opinions and attitudes towards reality and other people around us. This process is completely unconscious, therefore it's essential for us to recognize the source of our intentions, thoughts, emotions and actions. Being unaware of this hidden process causes us to be involuntarily filled with low-frequency energy, producing feelings of weakness, a lack of fulfillment, helplessness and exhaustion. At the same time, this attracts negative energy of low vibrations, which enhances our sensations and future life experiences.

If we are aware of the events, situations and coincidences in our life, it will help us understand that we are dealing with a great and hidden process whose impact is far beyond what we have imagined so far. Just by being aware of this hidden process and understanding that there are no coincidences in life and that nothing happens without a reason will start bringing us closer to the true source of power. We will start to attract positive energy that fills us with peace, harmony and love.

By recognizing at the deepest level the real and primary source of the energy underpinning your intentions and thoughts, you become capable of anticipating the consequences of your decisions and of making responsible choices. A responsible choice is one where, in a completely conscious manner, not distorted by sensual emotions, you are convinced of the true energy source of your intentions and thoughts. It is a manifestation of the greatest wisdom to be able to recognize the first thought triggering all subsequent ones, the one which determines the whole train of thought.

It is important to be aware that even the smallest negative intention or thought will determine the kind of energy that will support us in future. Even the tiniest negative intention or thought will rebound on us with great force. If you think about the great effects of small things, you realize that small and irrelevant things actually do not exist. You always have to pay attention to small things, because they can do the most harm. After all, it is possible for tiny bacteria to kill an entire big organism, a momentary lack of attention can end the greatest of lives or a small splinter in the foot can put a stop to even the longest journey. Those who do not notice small problems leave the door open for great tragedies to enter. An old proverb says that the biggest problems get through the smallest gap.

Destroy the seeds of evil within you before they grow and destroy you.

In keeping with the law of balance in the Universe, the energy that is the source of our intentions and thoughts will come back to us. In the world of energy, there is no principle of morality or judgment. These are the creations and interpretations of humankind. What carries a positive meaning in some circles can have a negative meaning in others. Life does not judge, but instead strives for an energy balance. What has been emitted will always come back. Sometimes you may have to wait a while, but there is no doubt it will return.

Being aware of this process facilitates making wise choices. Our energy always strives for a state of unity, that is, energy balance. Therefore, we must experience the effects of what we ourselves have previously created through our intentions, thoughts and actions. Any imbalance will make us create, in an absolutely unconscious way, the circumstances that make it possible for us to restore this balance in the future.

If our actions disturb another person's harmony, we can be certain that we will also experience such a disturbance. If, on the other hand, what we do makes the other person happy and is the source of power for them, we can also be sure that the same will happen to us. This principle allows us to experience what we cause and create ourselves, teaching us responsibility for our lives.

It is important to show understanding and compassion for each other, and not to judge a situation as bad or unfair, because it is certainly not unfair. All our life experiences foster our development and impact on us according to the way we interpret them. Their purpose is to heal and restore a perfect balance. Everything happens for a reason and always contains a higher good. The ability to link cause and effect fosters development and does not require us to go through the experience once again. Life is simple, the Universe always supports us with its full determination and with all its power with the kind of the energy we generate ourselves. That is why living a conscious life is an invaluable asset.

***

We are lucky to have been born in very favorable conditions. Happiness does not require wealth and everyone can be happy. External circumstances should not have any impact. Success should not lead to pride and arrogance and failure should not cause depression. We were endowed with the right to be happy at birth. Everyone can lead a happy life, as long as they are aware that their happiness comes from within, just as everyone can be filled with frustration and unhappiness, whilever they are convinced that this is an inherent part of their life, that this is their fate. Nature does not create shoddy goods, which is why at birth we were equipped with two tools to enable us to live a happy life:

consciousness and free will. Consciousness provides us with knowledge about the circumstances we find ourselves in, whereas free will allows us to make best possible choices. We can decide whether we want to remain in a given situation, change it or leave it. Most of the time, however, we do not use these tools, and instead we imagine that we have the power to change other people. This is a misconception. Nobody has the power to change another person. Therefore, everyone should work to improve themselves, not others - to change themselves, not others.

A person who is not aware thinks that it will make them feel better when somebody else changes.

Many people are permanently steeped in a negative mindset. They think of their lives as abnormally difficult: they can't succeed at anything, condemned to torment, failure and misfortune.

Why do so many people choose the "darker side of life"? Even their conversations most often deal with sad and pessimistic subjects. It is very rare for people to share their joy, passions and successes, and this way inspire each other. Most people go for what is bad, sad and depressing.

The roots of this unconscious way of living can be found in childhood. A child gains much more when he or she is unhappy. When the child is unhappy, everybody rushes to comfort them, to offer more compassion and love. Parents, family, siblings devote more of their time and attention, they focus more on the child. Such situations nourish the ego, give a sense of being important, and provide more energy.

Subconsciously, the child's mind learns this negative pattern: look unhappy and you will receive compassion and the attention of others; look sick and you will become the focus of interest. A sick child unwittingly becomes a young dictator: everyone gives way, the child's whims and desires are immediately fulfilled.

When a child is happy, nobody pays much attention. When the child is playing, when it is healthy and happy, nobody takes special care, nobody fulfills the child's whims.

Therefore, from the very beginning, many people unwittingly and completely unconsciously choose the worse, sad, pessimistic, darker side of life. If you are aware of this hidden pattern, you can start to change it. You should try to rely on yourself as much as possible and draw all your joy from within and not, in an unconscious way, seek the energy of compassion from other people.

All humans have free will and the right to decide for themselves how to think and act. The beauty and generosity of life is that everyone has the right to think independently and that no other can forbid this. People who think differently, who are aware of happiness, have a positive attitude to life and have faith in their lives can only offer empathy to those who have chosen another way of thinking and behaving. No one can be forced to change their way of thinking or behaving. No one has the right to insist that another person should change their way of thinking and live following the principles that we deem correct. If we truly wish to help another, we can only show through the example of our own life that it is possible to think and live differently, and not by offering advice. If somebody can't demonstrate this using their life as an example, then they certainly shouldn't be offering advice to others, as they will not only be unable to help anybody but even worse, they will only harm themselves. The world is full of teachers who have not yet found their own way but are all too ready to give directions to others.

You don't choose life, you just have to live it. But the way you do it is a matter of individual choice for each person. The role that we have been assigned by God (however you understand it) in the Theater of Life is irrelevant; what matters is the way we are going to play that part.

Do not attempt to appeal to others. Be yourself. You were born to be yourself. You have to strive to be who you truly are in order not to show a false face, not to poison your own energy system with fake energy. Otherwise, the same false energy will come back to you from others with double the force.

***

Every person strives for energy in a completely natural and unconscious way, because it is essential for living. Subconscious behavior resulting from an unconscious belief in the external nature of the origin of power often causes people to struggle for the part of energy that they have the easiest access to, the energy that flows between them.

Let's look at this issue from the inside, as it were, and reflect on how it is that in a completely unconscious way we may want to have an advantage or control over other people in order to acquire energy.

Quite often, after talking to someone we feel either energized or weakened. Subconsciously, the mind tries to manipulate others to capture their energy. Regardless of where the conversation takes place, the topic we are discussing or under what circumstances, more often than not we try, even completely unknowingly, to say something that will make us feel better, to come out as the winners. When our opinion comes out on top, we feel better emotionally, we are stronger and bolstered. The unconscious mind tries to defeat others not in order to achieve any success or arrive at a specific, pre-planned goal in the external world, but so that we feel great, so that we gain energy and feel more valuable. It is because of such hidden patters that there are so many irrational conflicts in the world. When during a conversation we gain "power, control" of another person, we take their energy. We feed ourselves at someone's expense. We completely unwittingly strive for "power and domination" over others, because we want to gain the energy that flows between people.

For instance, if we criticize a person who is weaker or dependent on us, and do so in an unpleasant or even aggressive manner, we make this person feel inferior and make them yield their energy to us. When such a person feels that their energy is being sapped, they have two options to recover it. They may explode with aggression in order to regain at least some of that energy and control. They can also close themselves in, become discontented and very aggrieved, which will trigger compassion in someone else or directly in the actual "aggressor". Thanks to this, they will regain their lost energy.

Another very common mechanism is to offer advice and guidance. A person who constantly gives all kinds of advice, guidance and instructions feels very good about it. They think they are so great and that they all do this out of care for others, for their benefit and safety. However, the root of such, even unconscious, behavior lies in the desire to take another person's energy. It is an unconscious way of showing who the smarter one is here and who knows better. If we show gratitude to such a person for their advice and guidance, they will feel great. If, on the other hand, we say, even in a very nice and polite way, that we don't need any advice or guidance, that we will manage on our own, this person will certainly feel worse, because they have failed to capture our energy.

And you, don't try to lecture others either. Nobody likes it, you included. Do you like being lectured by someone? It simply doesn't work and only creates unnecessary tension or stress. You won't help anyone and will hurt yourself. Listen to what others have to say, but never encroach on someone else's life without permission. All we can do is inspire others with our actions. There is nothing as beneficial as a good example. And always remember that you are the most important person in your life. If you are not there, you will certainly not help anyone and you will not set a good example.

Sometimes we ask someone in a very kind and warm way to do something for us. When the person refuses our heartfelt request, we feel bad about it, or even angry and upset. Why is it so?

It's because our request was not a request, it was actually a disguised demand. A true, sincere request always leaves room for refusal. Our ego very often takes on an extremely subtle form, but still remains an ego. Therefore, most often, in the guise of sweet words under the label "request" lies a hidden demand of the ego to fulfill its will.

Look at the world around you through others' eyes.

People who are perpetually dissatisfied, constantly in floods of tears and unhappy serve as another example of an unconscious process of triggering compassion in others in order to take over their energy.

Now and then we happen to come across someone who decides to give us their energy consciously and out of their own free will, at least for some time. Being around such a person makes us feel better and stronger. But this energy gift is not permanent and cannot last forever. No one is strong enough to sustain such a transfer of energy and unceasingly support another person, who with time treats such a transfer of energy as something completely natural, something they can take for granted, something unconditional and forever. Therefore, after some time, even the most romantic and wonderful relationship may turn into a tussle for power and for energy. The loser will always pay a high price. The person who was actively supporting their partner will begin to feel exploited, underappreciated and will view their actions as pointless. However, the person who was the recipient in this relationship usually starts to demonstrate their dissatisfaction, or surprised at the sudden change of the situation, even complains about not being supported like before. This person will grumble incessantly, as they will instinctively feel that something has been taken away from them, something to which they previously had an unconditional and eternal right.

Most people don't realize who much their good mood comes at somebody else's expense.

In a completely unconscious way, people compete with each other for the energy that they have the easiest access to, i.e. the energy flowing between them. This has always been and always will be the true source of all conflict. All such reactions stem from the need to fill an inner void, the need to overcome one's weaknesses or helplessness. At the root of this problem lies a deeply entrenched sense of a lack of self-esteem, and as a result, a lack of security.

When a person is weak, lacks self-confidence and self-esteem, they have to "steal" energy from somebody else. This is the easiest and yet, at the same time, the worst solution, because following the principle of balance, this kind of behavior will make the person experience events that will take place at their own expense.

When we try, even in an unconscious manner, to dominate or take control over another person, this person must consequently lose that control. In accordance with the law of cycles, we should expect to lose our control in the future, because the egoistic drive for dominance disturbs the natural balance and harmony of the Universe. We can be certain that this will happen. The only thing we don't know is where and when it will happen. Being aware of this hidden process and of the fact that the whole Universe is one big energy system will help us free ourselves from a constant, unconscious battle and the quest for other people's energy.

There is only one path to happiness and joy and that is to live in harmony with yourself. When you live in harmony with yourself, with your heart, spring is always within you, everything is in blossom and it also brings joy to all those around you.

> You will never be set free from what you
> remain silent about.

Everything we keep hidden deep inside as our secret is very harmful for us and has negative consequences. When we take it out into light of day, if it is something bad, it will disappear, dissolve in the daylight; if it is something good, it will bloom in the sun. If we hide something within ourselves, the opposite happens.

All good seeds wither when they lack contact with nature, and lack light. Such seeds can only bloom in sunlight, in contact with nature, which provides the right kind of energy. Bringing them out into the daylight makes them stronger, bigger, so that ultimately they bloom with all their might. If we keep them in the dark, they will become weaker and weaker over time until they finally dry out completely.

If we conceal something evil, it will grow within us. Evil does not need the light of day, it only grows in the dark, its kingdom is darkness. It will grow infinitely, destroying our psyche, bringing more and more sadness, fear and grief. In order to grow, it will sap all our energy and joy.

All that is brought to light becomes light itself.

Wherever competition and domination arise, violence appears. Every act of violence stems from the need to control and dominate other people. It makes no difference if it takes on an aggressive, tender or subtle form. Violence breeds violence. Every negative act triggers another. The only thing you need to remember is that the source of everything that happens to you in life always lies within you. Being able to see it this way is a difficult task, but it will transform your life. Arriving at an in-depth understanding of this covert process gives you access to the vast and inexhaustible power of the Spiritual Energy of the Universe, an understanding which is accessible for all, and doesn't come at the expense of another person or nature.

No progress can take place at the expense of another human being or nature. Both nature and other people's lives require the greatest respect. If we do not give them due respect and reverence, we cut ourselves off from the source of true power. Respect for these principles is the sole source and a natural source of true strength coming from the Spiritual Energy of the Universe. It brings harmony of heart and mind, self and soul. This is also the way for us to introduce the profoundest spiritual values into the material world. A good and strong person, endowed with authentic power, will not feel constrained nor in danger of losing their strong image if they show care for other people and nature. That is why such an attitude can only be adopted by strong and courageous people and the Universe will favor them. When all's said and done, the world belongs to the brave.

A life devoid of respecting other people and nature is not a natural state and leads to a rift with the ubiquitous Spiritual Energy of the Universe. Respecting the lives and dignity of others and of nature allows us to be wise and fair without the need for any choices or judgments. Nature does not judge. Judging is a subjective fabrication of the human imagination and has no counterpart in nature. Wisdom stemming from nature, which entails an absence of any judgment, teaches us to respect, and in turn means that care and empathy become part of our life at the expense of egotistical thinking. We begin to learn how to accept rather than judge. Judging is a kind of battle, and every battle leads to blindness, as such evaluations are made in the context of our own subjective values and experiences. True development, on the other hand, comes from accepting and not battling. Acceptance leads to profound, objective understanding, which fosters correct decision-making. Judging serves as a way to defend our own value system, which only leaves debris and ruin in its wake.

***

Telling others NO, living your own life, is not egotism. Egotism is demanding that others live the life that we believe to be the best; it is expecting others to live according to our preferences, for our pleasure, vanity or profit.

***

The fundamental desires for a sense of material and emotional security, for a sex life and a social life are appropriate and necessary to life. We brought these desires into the world with us, they are what make us human. These are natural instincts, which nature endowed us with. However, all too often these natural instincts essential to our life as humans are subject to degeneration. With great power, blindly and often extremely secretively and insidiously it governs us, stripping us of our self-control, stubbornly and steadfastly striving to rule our life. Overdeveloped, excessively unnatural needs become the cause of our problems. It's safe to say that almost every problem originates from a degeneration of our natural instincts. If we want our lives to be happy and in harmony with the Spiritual Energy of the Universe, it is extremely important that wish to establish precisely when and where our instincts were subject to degeneration; to analyze in a conscious, objective and thorough way when and in which circumstances they became a problem, a calamity, for ourselves, our loved ones or even complete strangers.

A rampant, unchecked sex drive is deeply rooted in a low sense of self-esteem and a lack of self-confidence; it stems from the unconscious intention of proving one's attractiveness and perfection to oneself. Devoid of any control whatsoever, it can destroy the emotional and material stability. Don't let desire take over. Rather than giving yourself over to the ephemeral pleasures of casual sex, seek lasting relationships.

The blind and beyond rational desire for a sense of material security leads to an extreme, where nothing provides pleasure or is of interest except for the accumulation of money and material valuables. In the pursuit of the external world's goods we often forget what we really need. Joy, a love of life, spiritual calm, inner harmony – none of this can come from the outside. You have to rediscover what is within you, what you were born with, your inner nature, which can never be lost. For this reason, whenever the desire to possess something appears in our mind, we should give great consideration to whether we are not paying too high a price for it. Poor and unhappy are those who are unable to appreciate what they have, and preoccupy themselves with what they would like to have. It is not who have little who are poor, but rather those who have too little. Many people believe that if they gain or achieve this or that, they'll be able to care for themselves or their loved ones, and live a happy and peaceful life. Unfortunately, such people are most often found in cemeteries.

Don't think about accumulating wealth for old age. This is the wrong approach. Happiness cannot be put off until later. Learn to live in the moment. Nobody knows how much time they have left.

Don't be a slave to material possessions. In the excessive pursuit of the material world's goods, dazzled by vanity, dreams of greatness and glory, we can, in an entirely unconscious way, become utterly blind to our own weaknesses and the needs of our nearest and dearest. We might possess everything we wish for in life, but this will not fill the inner void. Until we understand this, we will always feel we are lacking something and remain poor.

The irrational pursuit of a feeling of security can also express itself in a non-material form, as dependence on another person. This is primarily related to the lack of responsibility for one's own life and the desire to shift this responsibility onto somebody else. This kind of behavior evidently leads to recurrent disappointment and frustration. Nobody has the right to burden another with responsibility for their life. However many times we attempt to do so, it will always end in problems and unhappiness. By demanding that others devote excessive attention to us or if we lose control of our egotistic need for recognition and appreciation, in matters of lesser or greater importance, we lead to resentment being shown towards us. The result is that people simply start to avoid us. Our insatiable hunger for glorification will bring about an explosion of anger and aversion.

If we start to exploit and buffet others in our blind pursuit of our own interests, we will trigger their anger, rage and vindictiveness. Every departure from what is natural causes conflict, not only with other people, but also with ourselves. If we are unaware of this degeneration of our natural instincts and unable to cope with it, we will never achieve inner peace and harmony.

***

I am entirely responsible for my own life.
Understanding this simple statement liberates you from feelings of hurt, resentment and grudges. By liberating yourself from these negative feelings, you make your life healthier.

He who wants, looks for ways,
he who does not want, looks for reasons.

When the wish to take prevails over the wish to give, or when the desire to give, or the wish for a sense of security, whether emotional or material, deprives another of this, we disrupt the energy order of the Universe, which in turn removes the natural defense that our life provides. This starts the emanation of negative energy, which automatically draws in energy vibrating on the same frequencies. We can expect that in order to maintain the Universe's energy equilibrium, we will experience circumstances to our cost. The Universe is an ideal, harmonious, self-regulating system that always striving for the highest level of balance. It teaches us the way of respecting others and responsibility for our actions. Respecting is not the same as respect. Respect is a subjective evaluation and is related to the values we represent or which were programmed into us by our environment. That is why respect is a subjective value. That which stimulates the greatest respect in one environment might have the entirely opposite significance in another, and might even be regarded as something reprehensible. Respect is an artificial value and does not exist in an objective form. However, respecting the values preached by others without evaluating them is a feature that derives from a positive energy source, and engenders positive emanations, which in turn attract similar vibrations to us.

It is the degree of respecting others that determines the limit of our true power. A lack of respecting values is both a source of consent to abuse others and an obstacle to achieving true strength drawn from the boundless ocean of the Spiritual Energy of the Universe. Respecting is a program on which we build our future experiences in our relations with others. We are the ones to decide what we will experience with them. When we are aware of our thoughts and actions, we are able to predict their consequences.

> Don't try to control what does not
> depend on you.

Unconscious inclinations to control our surroundings and external factors to our own benefit also lead to becoming reliant on pleasant sensations reaching us from outside. These might be manifested in a whole range of addictions, such as alcohol, drugs, sex, shopping, food, other people, etc. All these habits are connected with an addiction to pleasant sensations caused by external factors and are evidence of the lack of ability to derive joy from life from within ourselves.

Most often we find excuses for ourselves, saying "I can't do that" or "I can't cope with that". These are typical tricks of the mind. Their aim is to pass the buck, to place responsibility for our life outside ourselves, and at the same time, to give ourselves permission for any undesirable behavior. This is the easiest and simplest way to do it, but unfortunately, it is not possible to cast off responsibility for our own intentions, thoughts and actions. We are the ones who will experience most the consequences of our decisions and choices, which is why we must rise above all these mechanisms and learn to listen to our inner voice flowing from the depths of our heart. Full of love and belief, this voice never lies and is not distorted by a constantly calculating and cold mind, lined with fear and uncertainty. Only decisions that are made consciously and which take into account their long-term consequences safeguard us against behaving improperly. They help us understand that the true source of strength is within us. It is connected with the limitless ocean of the Spiritual Energy of the Universe. But we only have access to this when our decisions are made in line with the voice of a heart filled with love and empathy, when the values we profess foster our development, with no negative impact on others or on nature. These professed values are the ones truly reflected in our lives, in how we behave from one day to the next. All that matters is what we really do and not what we think, or what we'd like to do. A tree is judged by its fruits and not by its roots. Life does not hold us accountable for our intentions and thoughts but for our actual deeds.

If we shut ourselves off from our true feelings, we close off access to the life-giving Spiritual Energy of the Universe, the source of our positive thoughts and actions, which form the basis of future life experiences. This is why it is important to live and do everything in accordance with our nature, listening to our own heart. Don't follow advice, follow your own heart. This is the best piece of advice. If we learn to listen carefully and consciously, we will never go wrong. By listening to your heart, you slowly begin to head in the right direction, not thinking about what is good or bad.

If we are unable to listen to our inner voice, and yet still live in harmony with what others ask or expect from us, while not thinking about their own true inner self, we lose the connection with the energy flowing from the depths of our heart, which is inextricably linked with the Spiritual Energy of the Universe. As a result, we become susceptible to and capable of evil deeds emanating from the darkest recesses of our unconscious mind. All our negative behaviors are evidence that we have lost contact with the Spiritual Energy of the Universe, the energy of our heart, which is incapable of bad deeds.

The strong are generous, the weak are stern.

All our actions are underpinned by our intentions. It is these that determine their effects and their impact on us, going far beyond the boundaries of the physical world. If we are unable to make ourselves aware of the true sources of our intentions, we are in no position to associate our negative experiences with their causes. If we are not able to make contact with our intentions, emotions and feelings, we are incapable of empathy and sympathy. Awareness of our own thoughts and emotions and the ability to gain a clear insight into them reveals the intentions within. Awareness of emotions leads to an awareness of intentions. It is precisely this rift between emotions, feelings and intentions that produces a lack of internal harmony and of emotional stabilization. If we really love somebody, but the deep, unconscious source of this feeling is the fear of being alone, we are not in a position to maintain emotional stability and internal harmony, since a rift exists between our emotions and our intentions. The true answer to the question of "Do I love or do I need?" requires great courage, but certainly generates a lesser internal rift. It is extremely significant whether our guide in everything we do in life is faith or fear. Do our actions stem from a source of joy and faith, or are they underpinned by fear of loss or of the situation worsening. Belief is an inner conviction that things will be the way we want them to be, and not a hidden or fear-filled plea for help addressed to some higher being. It does not contain a single grain of negative energy. Ideas that are based on belief are always directed towards the positive and in no way refer to negative reminiscences or events. Actions based on fear stem from negative sources. Their power is the fear of loss, a desire to improve something we are dissatisfied with, and a fear of returning to negative memories or events. Belief in action means everything we do is aimed at the light side, whereas fear-based actions are directed as far from darkness as possible. The direction may be the same, but the actions are based on two opposing energy sources. The kind of energy we use determines our actions: we will either be supported by positive energy, causing actions to be filled with lightness and joy, or everything will be an uphill struggle, bought by great hardship. As a consequence, instead of joy they will cause constant depression. Those whose actions stem from fear are rarely happy with what they have, but rather worry about what they might lose. Fear of loss dominates over the joy of possessing. Thought is energy, energy is vibrations, and vibrations attract the same vibrations. This is why it is so important whether we are guided by belief or fear.

It is precisely for these reasons that it is worth giving careful consideration to the consequences of our intentions, thoughts and actions before making any kind of choice. Conscious observation of our own feelings and sensations will prove helpful in doing so. If we feel any tension or any other disharmony within ourselves, this means that we are doing something at odds with our inner self, incompatible with the energy of our heart. This is an indication of our disrupting the balance in the Spiritual Energy of the Universe. Such a state can only regain equilibrium through personally experiencing the consequences of our own behavior.

In conjunction with a deep understanding and consciousness of the unceasing, hidden and all-pervading process of striving for a state of balance, we begin to sense discomfort in taking any decision that might prove inappropriate and harmful to others, with consequences for ourselves.

***

Parable / Metaphor:

Two angels, one older and one younger were walking through the wilderness. Before dusk, a beautiful palace appeared in front of their eyes. They knocked on the door and asked the owner to put them up for the night. The owner, however, did not invite them in, and instead pointed at a run-down room at the back of the stables, adjacent to a rock, as a place for them to stay overnight. In this room, there was a crack in the wall on the rock side, which the senior angel repaired in the morning. The younger angel asked his older friend why he'd done it, for after all, the owner was a very wealthy man, though he hadn't even invited them into his palace, nor provided them with food, but instead had sent them to sleep in the old room, which he himself never even visits. The older one only said: "Nothing is as it seems".

In the morning, they set off on their journey again. In the evening, they came across an old, tumbledown hut where a poor, elderly couple lived. They knocked on the door and asked about staying overnight. These good-hearted, elderly people invited them in with great kindness, served them dinner and gave them their own bed to sleep in, while they themselves went to sleep in the kitchen. In the morning, the younger angel heard huge despair coming from the hosts in kitchen. After a while, he found out that their only cow had died that night. He asked the older angel why he had not protected the cow belonging to these kind and friendly people. The older angel merely said: "Nothing is as it seems".

The younger angel said he didn't understand any of this and asked his senior colleague to explain why he had renovated the room of a rich yet cunning and unwelcoming man the previous night, while tonight he hadn't saved the only cow that belonged to the kindly, old people. The senior angel explained, "Yesterday, when I woke up, I went up to a crack in the wall of the room where we slept, and saw through it old cave behind the wall full of ancient treasures. I decided to fix the wall so that the rich but wicked man would not be able to find them. But today I woke up at night and saw that Death came to these kind people's house to take the elderly man's wife, and all I could do was trade her for a cow.

Remember: Nothing is as it seems.

***

The synthesis of the latest discoveries in physics, quantum physics and psychology, mystical and religious messages irrefutably confirm the existence of a process that is uniform, invisible and far beyond the capabilities of cognition. This is why, in everything we do, it is better to assume that the Spiritual Energy of the Universe exists, for even if we are mistaken in this, we certainly have nothing to lose in assuming so.

***

You are limited only
by your own beliefs.

***

The world that surrounds you and your
inner world are like two wings of one bird.
If a bird has one strong wing and
the other one is weak,
it will never be able to fly.

***

CONSCIOUSNESS

Let's start by understanding what consciousness is. As you live your life, you become aware of many things in the world around you. You are conscious of everyday matters, your desires, responsibilities, goals, needs, the people around you and reality. But are you aware of yourself? Are you conscious of the needs of your heart, aware of what is happening inside you, in the world of your feelings and emotions?

Just as you observe the outside world, start to observe what is happening within you, in your inner world. An awareness that extends in both directions will deepen your understanding of yourself. Your reactions and behavior will become more conscious, and take into account their impact on your inner world, the world of your sensations, emotions and feelings. Having this awareness not only of what surrounds you but also of what is happening inside you will enable you to distance yourself from the reality around you and look at it from a different, more conscious perspective.

The hardest thing is to know yourself, which is why few have an awareness of the needs of their own heart, their own desires and emotions. Most of the time we know ourselves in terms of what others think or say about us. They say: you are a superb tailor, manager, cook, salesperson, engineer, teacher, etc. However, by identifying ourselves with their assessment of us, we forget about our true self. In other people's opinions, just as in a mirror, our own image is reflected. But they know only our exterior. This is the root of the inner dualism, the cause of our feeling internally torn and lost. The gulf between who we really are in the depths of our hearts and whether we identify with others' perception of us widens from one moment to the next.

Our personality is a reflection of the energy that rules within us. It is a manifestation of the internal balance between our inner world and what we identify with. You cannot live in harmony when detached from this balance. By taking care of our spiritual development, we foster our personality's development. It is impossible to function properly in the outside world while completely forgetting about our own spiritual development. The idea that it is possible to function in the real world detached from this balance is a misconception that might result in mental illness or push us towards different means of changing our consciousness, such as alcohol, drugs or psychotropic drugs. Our emotional state is directly proportional to the state of this balance. A lack of balance and harmony in life is solely the consequence of an inner schism, and if we want our life to be coherent and harmonious, we must eliminate the cause, which lies inside us. If we fail to do this, we will have to bear the consequences. There is simply no other way. We are responsible for the schism here. We ourselves create this inner rift.

Life means evolution, development, constant motion. Unconscious evolution ends with humans and conscious evolution begins. However, it starts only when we ourselves decide that it should start. You cannot stand still, because life moves forward, so when you stay in the same place, you go backwards. We can either evolve to a higher state of consciousness or go backwards. This choice is up to each and every one of us. Most people don't choose conscious progress: they stand still, not knowing what they want, where to go, not even realizing in which direction they are moving. They live in an illusory world of the imagination or seek to return to the past and oblivion. They look for this in fruitless social encounters, in work, alcohol, drugs, sex and countless addictions to sensual pleasure. Only very few continue their journey to the higher levels of consciousness. The conscious choice to develop is a great adventure, the best that can happen to any person.

> To become a better person you don't need
> to wait for others to change.

By loving yourself, you take the first steps towards developing consciousness, for this is the path to your heart, to knowing yourself, without the external conditioning of the mind. Those who do not love themselves will always have problems with self-awareness. The mind will always pull them away from this path, telling them it is meaningless, nonsense. It will invent dozens of reasons to drag them away from the path of self-knowledge. After all, it functions almost like a representative of the society in which we live and does not allow for any individual behavior that could threaten to move away from the conditions imposed by that society. Consciousness means setting aside the mind's conditioning and observing reality as it is, without the distortions caused by external factors that have conditioned our mind. By loving yourself and being conscious of your own self, you begin to cleanse yourself of many external factors that have been programmed into you. You become free of these conditions.

> It's better to go part of the way along the right road than go further, but down the wrong road.

To function properly, our body, mind and our entire inner workings require love's energy. We upset the harmony of this energy if our actions are devoid of love. If we bottle up our negative emotions, we harm ourselves and others.

***

As consciousness develops, the views we have held so far begin to lose their relevance to be replaced by new ones, just as the discovery of electricity left humanity dissatisfied with candlelight. Yet the benefits of electricity did not make candles worthless or useless. This is exactly what progress is. Something must go away in order for there to be room for something new.

But there is no need to worry - truth and good will remain forever. These are eternal and timeless.

**

Let's imagine that our consciousness is a horse pulling a cart containing everything that is connected with our external, material world.

There's no doubt that the only intelligent and right way is for the horse to stand in front of the cart. The more care we take of the horse, the stronger it will be and the bigger the carriage it will be able to pull. What's more, such an arrangement lets him see everything in front of him, right up to the horizon. Seeing everything around him will allow him to choose the straightest, best and easiest route. A strong horse choosing the easier and shorter path will pull a very big cart with no difficulty. If, on the hand, we put the horse behind the cart, which is definitely not the correct and natural arrangement, we will cause the horse to tire very quickly by pushing even a small cart, not to mention that it will see nothing except the cart. In places, he will push it along a very bumpy, uneven road, not even seeing that right alongside is a beautifully flat and straight road.

If we want to fix our lives, we should remember that the only correct arrangement is for the horse to always be in front of the cart. Spiritual progress always goes before material wealth, never the other way around. But that doesn't mean that you have to renounce anything.

**

The human mind consists of the conscious and the unconscious, with the unconscious mind lying just behind consciousness. Sometimes we can hear its very quiet voice, but it is difficult to make it out. It is this unconscious mind that pulls the strings, mysteriously and incomprehensibly determining our behavior. It seems to us that we make our decisions consciously, but in fact we only make those decisions within the bounds of what the unconscious mind permits us to do. This is where we find the seeds from which our "conscious" behavior grows.

The unconscious part is the largest area in our mind and comprises the unconscious associated with our lives and the multi-generational unconscious. The conscious part is only the tip of the iceberg of all those elements that have conditioned our mind. The way we think and act is the result of processes taking place in both the personal and multi-generational parts of our unconscious. It may seem to us that we think and act consciously, but it really all depends on the unconscious. To make this process easier to understand, let's imagine that our mind is a computer - a bio-computer with an operating system such as Windows or iOS. These operating systems are our unconsciousness, the personal and multi-generational parts. Our consciousness, on the other hand, is an application that works in the way the operating system, i.e. unconsciousness, allows it to. Next, let's imagine that our consciousness is, for example, a text editor - let's call it Word. When we work on the computer, we use Word without paying attention to the operating program it works on.

However, our Word program will behave how the Windows or iOS operating system allows it to. If there's a bug in the operating system, no attempt to repair Word will succeed, because the problem lies deeper, in the operating system itself. We can change, repair or modify our applications continually, but until we deal with the operating system, they will all work badly or incorrectly. The same goes for our consciousness. We receive different kinds of signals from outside and all the information related to this signal passes through our whole mind. All these external signals move through the conscious and the unconscious. The unconscious mind processes this information in line with its conditioning and passes it on to the conscious part, which in turn reacts accordingly. The way we act is not the result of information that has come to us from outside; rather, it is the result of information that has come from the unconscious mind to the conscious part. It is this information from the unconscious that determines all our actions. What is unconscious has a greater impact on the way we think and act than what is conscious.

It's hardest to defeat the enemy living
inside your own head.

The unconscious part relates to and contains everything that has happened in our lives - all our memories from the past, including those that we ourselves produced, and those we do not remember nor even want to remember, because we are ashamed of them. This is all part of the conditioning programmed into our lives when we were developing as children. This conditioning shaped our mind in terms of our beliefs, as well as our religious, cultural and environmental views. Its purpose is not to serve us, but the society we grew up and live in. If you are a Christian, your mind works the way Christianity wants it to. If you are Hindu, your mind is Hindu. If you are a Muslim, your mind is Muslim. If you have grown up among in atheist and cosmopolitan society that rejected spiritual needs, your mind defines you as such. Reality is neither Christian, nor Hindu, nor Muslim, neither rich nor poor. Reality is as it is.

This part also contains all the unpleasant external situations we have experienced and which are the cause of unpleasant or traumatic memories. To a great extent this part is determined by all situations and circumstances that occurred in our childhood. Such situations caused us great suffering as children, and a child's defense mechanism casts them into the unconscious in order to safeguard this innocent little creature from anguish. Very often these are situations that we have no recollection of in our adult life.

Whenever we witness a situation or somebody's behavior, or when we hear an opinion or opinion that resonates with what is in our unconscious, we become irritated, react very negatively or descend into extremes of emotion. This is because the situation has met its counterpart in our lives. The principle of resonance aroused something within us that we are ashamed of, do not wish to remember, or which is inconsistent with what was programmed into us, and does not necessarily accord with who we really are deep in our hearts. According to this principle, nothing can stimulate any response in us if its source does not lie within us. The potency of our reaction depends on how numerous these elements are and how strongly we have concealed them.

The unconscious mind produces immense chaos, which leads us to misinterpret everything. We see only what we want to see, and we hear only what we want to hear. The unconscious mind notices something pleasurable on the horizon. It glorifies this and interprets it as a great value worth striving for. We proceed in this direction utterly blinded and lost in illusions of eternal happiness once we achieve our goal. When difficulties arise, anger, rage and dissatisfaction begin to appear. How often do our dreams not fit in with reality! In the unconscious part of our mind, we create unreal images. Without understanding a situation, we unconsciously ascribe it a particular meaning, and when reality turns out to be different, everything bursts like a bubble, causing us to descend into depression and despair.

> Pride and vanity change even the most noble intentions into the reverse.

Why does our conscious mind shove everything negative into the unconscious? Because in our consciousness we are so marvelous and wonderful.

Now let's imagine that there's a narrow passage between our consciousness and unconsciousness where we cast everything that is unwanted in our consciousness. Then we quickly shut the door to this passageway and place a warden there to guard the entrance. His task is to ensure that this door always remains closed and not to allow anything to get back into our consciousness. This warden is our ego, whose job it is to maintain our conviction of how wonderful we are. However, our unconsciousness has no interest in keeping these negative memories inside. It would be willing to get rid of them, to move them to consciousness, and to liberate us from them in a conscious way. The problem is that the guard, our ego, does not want to hear a word about them or even look at them. So, if a situation or someone's words really hit home, right on the door to our unconsciousness and resonate with something we are concealing there, our warden is momentarily stunned, lets down his guard and the door opens. Whatever we are concealing there starts to get out. After a while, however, the guard, our ego, is back at full strength and with huge determination attempts to close the door, and in doing so triggers extreme emotions whose sole purpose is to jam the signals coming out of the unconscious.

Nothing from outside can upset us if its source does not lie within us.

When somebody's behavior unleashes negative emotions in us, it means that the source of these emotions also lies within us. If we want to change this, we should give great thought to just how old the little child within us really is, and what hidden experiences that we either can't remember or don't wish to are behind this reaction. We can change this situation if we identify and understand the sources of these emotions in the experiences and actions of our past. If we succeed in doing this, we can start the healing process, which will have a positive impact on our life to come, free us from the memories rooted in our unconscious mind.

Now, let's look at the unconscious, multi-generational conditioning of the mind. In order to better understand how the conditioning of a person's mind and thoughts have changed in a multi-generational time-space, let's try to imagine that happens within one person's lifetime. Such a perspective will make it easier for us to understand why we see the world in one way and not another. By tuning into what people thought and felt in bygone times, it will be easier to understand our own unconscious, multi-generational mind conditioning.

Let's start out by imagining that we are living in very distant times. Our world and the reality we live in are strictly described and defined by our spiritual leaders, who wield immense power and profound influence over our minds. It is they who create our reality, based on some divine plan or other, which they and only they understood and prescribed. The life-giving force of the Sun, the ominous volcanoes, the unbridled power of the oceans were all seen as signs of our gods. Our leaders presented us with images of various gods, around which all manner of myths were spun. These images had secret, magic power. Their role was to ward off danger and ensure prosperity. They played a crucial role in our beliefs and rituals, whether as objects of devotion or fear. Our spiritual leaders explained how we were the chosen ones and had been placed at the very center of the Universe purely to enjoy salvation after death. It was thanks to them that we knew how to live our lives in order to pass the spiritual examination. We had absolutely no doubt about that. At that time, we were constantly forced to choose between two diametrically opposed forces of the gods and demons. Our ancestors were the ones to tell us whether our behavior was in line with the wishes of the gods or whether we had been deceived by demons. If we obeyed their orders, we were certain of the reward awaiting us after our death. However, if we strayed from the path they had laid out for us, we were sure to be cursed and condemned to eternal damnation. Each and every aspect of our lives was defined in spiritual and supernatural terms. Anything good we encountered in our lives was defined as a gift from the gods. This reinforced the conviction that we were living life in accordance with the rules set out by our leaders. However, if something bad occurred, it was evidence that we had strayed and fallen into the devil's clutches. In the air, in the sky, on the ground, and beneath it - everywhere we suspected hostile forces were lying in wait for us, ready to annihilate us if we didn't follow the laws set by our leaders. It was they who sought the grace of our gods through prayer, witchcraft, spells or sacrifice. The bloodier the sacrifice, the more it appeased the gods, which is why the altars of the primeval gods dripped with the blood of animal and human sacrifices. Death was omnipresent and not a source of dread. We fully accepted the existence of good and evil in the world around us, which paradoxically enabled us to enjoy every moment of life. All phenomena, from hurricanes, earthquakes and solar eclipses through to the death of loved ones were attributed to God's will or the malice of demons. We were utterly convinced that the world was ruled by divine laws as interpreted by our spiritual leaders. Such concepts as climate, tectonic plates or diseases simply did not feature in our imaginations. Our leaders were the sole intermediaries between ourselves and the gods we believed in, and we believed that they wielded absolute power over our lives. We believed that we were destined to remain forever in the social class we had been born into. Our ego could not entertain the thought that we might enjoy greater wealth or achievements. If we were born in an impoverished village, we never talked of buying a beautiful new house. Our position in society was secondary to the spiritual reality shaped by our rulers. We had no doubts or dilemmas as to our beliefs or our role on Earth. For a deeper understanding of this, we need to identify with our primeval ancestors' way of thinking.

The next stage of our lives saw us begin to meet those who had traveled the world. It was they who told us of other regions, of people who believe in different gods to ours, of different customs and a different way of looking at life. We listened to these tales with great surprise, as it called into question all the beliefs we had held up till then. What's more, scientists and astronomers provided conclusive proof that the Sun and stars do not orbit the Earth, as our leaders had maintained. The earth proved to be merely a small planet in an immense Universe. We lost our position at the center of the divine world, a fact that was irreversible. We became uncertain and were led to question our unique position. Science began to flourish, raising questions related to tectonic plates, vegetation, how diseases start and how they develop. Increasing numbers of people started to travel and engage in trade. Buying goods in other parts of the world and selling in another, they became ever wealthier before our eyes. We saw how we are able to change our social status and become richer. The interpretation of the world and our place within it that we had held until that point was called into question. The leaders we had followed so far lost their credibility, our unquestioning belief in them ceased and yet at the same time, by focusing on the real world, we felt disorientated. This came as a huge blow. Our world quite literally came crashing down before our very eyes. We were plagued by questions of truth, and how to define the meaning of life. Our worldview collapsed irreversibly, we lost all confidence. Everything we had believed up to that point needed to be reinterpreted. We stopped accepting without question the spiritually based depiction of the Universe put forward by our leaders, and began to challenge our authority figures. Doubting these spiritual leaders, and had no desire for them to control our lives. Our faith in them was lost, never to be regained, and with it, the belief in their portrayal of a world ruled by God. Yet we ourselves were unable to provide explanations for everything, in particular the spiritual meaning of existence. For this we would need help. Luckily, science had appeared and begun to develop, and we placed absolute trust in it. Science was to analyze the world, discover how it works, and tells us why we are living in it. Scholars were to provide answers to our questions about the world around us and the true meaning of our existence, while not excluding the essence of God. Unfortunately, the world proved to be too complex and scientific methods disappointingly insufficient. Scientists were unable to explain the purpose of our existence and our relations with God. The lack of any answer to these fundamental questions had a powerful impact on our further lives. We came to the conclusion that as we do not understand the meaning of our spiritual existence and are unable to find an answer to the most important questions, we should concentrate instead on the here and now. We stopped concerning ourselves with the spiritual sphere and focused on the material world. The issue of spiritual growth was sidelined, pushed aside until it was finally forgotten completely. We stopped worrying about being spiritually lost.

> The majority of people have enough religion
> in them to hate, but not enough to love.

Our goal became the pursuit of achievements in the material world, a goal in itself, but one lacking in depth. We completely lost ourselves in the creation of material security, which was to replace spiritual security. A life of sensual pleasure and the best material conditions became our goal. Materialism and consumerism dominated our lives, which boiled down to nothing more than practical matters. Money became the god above all others, the only god, the one we believe in most. The God of Commerce took over our lives.

Observing how human consciousness has evolved in recent centuries, we can notice how it has led to an obsession with growth in material terms, with a total disregard for spiritual needs.

No doubt many will pose the question: "How does the multi-generational evolution of the human consciousness affect the conditioning of my multi-generational unconscious mind?"

As I wrote in Chapter One, everything is energy. It is worth considering how this multi-generational energy might be transferred to us and how we receive it.

A receiver is required to capture any form of energy. Radio waves are everywhere, but to capture them it is essential to have a receiver working on the same frequency. An example of such a receiver is a radio set, which processes energy in the form of sound, which in turn is picked up by another receiver, the human ear. It is thanks to this receiver that we can hear sound. We could also assume that a receiver capable of picking up the multi-generational energy of the growth in human consciousness is a woman's fertilized egg.

***

Don't believe something just because you were told to believe it. Don't blindly follow the crowd, because you won't go any further than the crowd does. Listen to the opinions of others, but let yourself have your own opinions, thought and beliefs. Humanity owes all its development only to those who had their own opinions and thought differently.

We attract everything around us. We create everything around us by means of our thoughts. We are responsible for what we think about, how we do this, and how we use our energy. Decisions made under the influence of negative emotions are the most harmful ones and consume the most energy. That is why you have to be continuously aware of your thoughts. We are the ones who create our own reality. Our thoughts create our truth.

To understand better how we function, let's imagine that our unconscious mind and heart are two departments in a company called Our Life. If the management board of Our Life is located the unconscious mind, the company will be guided by extreme, vacillating visions of a perfectly happy life and great calamities. We will find ourselves buffeted by mood swings. Of course, from time to time the management located in the unconscious mind will heed the signals emitted from the Heart department and meet its needs, but only on its own terms. The Heart's needs will not be fully taken into account in its decisions.

Our mind, our thought process and consequently our behavior is highly complex. The mind is not homogeneous and consists of what might be called the 'mind board'. Let's imagine this mind board is a government consisting of a Council of Ministers comprising different ministers with their own independent voting rights. This Council of Ministers includes such ministers as the Minister for Anger and Wrath, the Minister for Memories, the Minister for Conditioning the Unconscious Mind, the Minister for

Fantasy Future Planning, the Minister for Envy, the Minister for Greed and Coveting, and the Minister for Combat and Conflict Creation. The Council of Ministers has its own Chairperson, who has the casting vote. This Chairperson is the Pure Consciousness, which represents the needs of our Heart, the needs of our inner, spiritual world. Unfortunately, it is usually the case that this Chairperson sleeps through Council of Ministers meetings and his vote is not taken into account. Now let us imagine that some external factors have given a boost, for example, to the Minister of Greed and Coveting. Then, blinded by the needs of their Ministry, he or she begins to convince all the other Ministers that the best and most beneficial solution for our lives is to act in accordance with his or her plans. Meanwhile, the Chairperson, the Pure Consciousness, representing the needs of our heart and our inner world, lies in a slumber and does not present to the other Ministers the long-term influence and impact of the actions taken by the Minister of Greed and Coveting, for this Minister's wonderful visions win over the other members of the Council of Ministers with ease. A similar situation occurs when any of the other ministers speaks.

What's more, in the absence of its Chairman, the Pure Consciousness, the Council of Ministers has a compulsion to judge others, criticize and organize the world, dividing it into good and bad, distinguishing in the world that which is "liked and disliked", "wanted and unwanted". Each of these Ministers has a very strong ego, and the moment it is attacked in any way, be this attack real or imagined, then all Ministers, driving each other on, are ready to unite against everyone and everywhere, without a thought for the consequences.

As this visualization shows, it is crucial for us to be constantly aware of our actions, to take into account their long-term impact on our inner world, the world of our heart. If the casting vote in Our Life is held by the Pure Consciousness, representing our inner needs, then we are able to achieve everything in life. It is enough for the Chairperson of the Council of Ministers to "command" all other ministers to follow this line of thought and this course of action in order to achieve the goals set by the Chair.

If the Pure Consciousness is a constant presence in our life, all conflicts arising so far will come to an end. Nobody will succeed in dragging us into any conflict, no matter how hard they try.

A fully conscious person is able to express their opinion clearly and emphatically, but does not invest any energy in it that might prompt any reaction. Without adopting a defensive or offensive stance, and by not attacking anyone, they do not cause any conflicts. Being conscious and internally integrated, you do not generate any conflicts. You no longer have to defend the interests of your ego: my right, my territory, my idea, my will, etc. This applies to conflicts with others, but above all to inner conflict, which ceases when there is no longer any friction between the demands and expectations of your programmed unconscious mind.

Trust your intuition, take the road your heart shows you to follow and you will see that you are much stronger than you think.

Half of the people accept the inner, spiritual world, and deny the existence of the material world. They have condemned the body and matter, calling it an illusion. For them the outside world is unimportant - it does not exist. Having renounced this world, they remain poor, sick and starving. The other half accept the material world, but deny the existence of the inner world, the spiritual world. These people have stopped attending to their own inner world, and have rejected spiritual needs. They have turned all their attention outwards, to a pleasure-filled, hedonistic life, lacking any depth, and mainly for show. In the world of possessions, they constantly strive not to be left behind. This illusion of a pleasant life has resulted in unprecedented sales of psychotropic drugs and antidepressants. These people take huge amounts of drugs, narcotics - mainly alcohol and drugs - to stifle their inner needs, not to hear how their own heart cries. They play, sing and dance in a crowd, in a crowd of lonely people, but mourn their fate in solitude.

In both cases, we speak of halves, and someone who is a half cannot be happy. Life consists of the internal and external. Only by nurturing true growth in both these elements will we make ours a full and harmonious life. We should care for sensual pleasures to the same extent as we do spiritual ones.

If we devote too much attention to one of these elements, it will be at the expense of the other, which in turn will disrupt our internal harmony and cause an imbalance in the Spiritual Energy of the Universe. Happiness is a state of perfect balance between the sensual and spiritual worlds, and has nothing to do with pleasures supplied only from outside. If we do not achieve a state of balance based on these two equally important pillars, nothing from the outside can make our lives peaceful and happy. For a life to be happy, it must be complete, not just a half. It must be whole, taking advantage of all the benefits of the external, material world in a spiritual way. Love yourself, take care of your inner self and make full use of life. But don't let what's outside take hold of you, so that the desire to possess becomes your goal. This will create your own inner hell.

If you have a goal in life that really is extremely important to you, you will always find the right road. However unattainable this goal might be, there is always a way to overcome the obstacles in reaching it. Your motivation determines the success of your actions. It is crucial whether you will be guided by faith or fear. Sometimes a hint of craziness is also needed. Believe that you can, and you will have already made it half way.

Eternal deceit of nature. The mirage of beauty
that puts the alert mind to sleep.

There can be no doubt that money is important, but it cannot be the goal. Work is essential to satisfy obvious material needs, but a balanced approach to it is necessary. It's nice to have a good car, a beautiful home, but it is important to remember that more precious values exist. The human mind is exceptionally cunning. Noticing the prospect of becoming wealthier or of experiencing pleasure, it interprets this as a value whose consequence is greed, which leads us to lose ourselves in our delusions. Workaholism, the blind pursuit of money – this is a very unhealthy approach, the root cause of numerous problems, including a weakening of relations with our nearest and dearest, and even this closeness waning entirely. At this point, relations based on material foundations emerge, and in time become the sole binding force. Looking around, it appears that everything has been turned upside down. So many people seem to live to satisfy the needs of their bank accounts, hoarding money and then dying. They live as if it was the house that needed them, that they are working for their house's needs. The discriminate against spiritual needs, regard those who have 'dropped out of the race to enrichment' as feckless and lazy. After all, it's really that these did not even start to live, imprisoned in routine and the sense of safety. They never experienced the joy of life in full, not even for a moment.

We should bear in mind that humans also have spiritual needs. If we lose sight of these, we become robots, and the intimacy in our relationships dies away. If you are capable of relaxing, letting go and not engaging in the chase, you have a healthy attitude to life. Allow yourself to be inactive for a moment, to sit in peace and quiet. Enjoy the birdsong, the noise of the wind. Silence like this enables you to tune into the music of the Universe. Cast into a state of suspension at the sight of the sunrise and sunset, it will suddenly dawn on you just how beautiful these are.

> The happiness from interacting with people is superficial. The happiness that is born when you are alone is immensely deep.

Every person functions with their head or heart as the intermediary. If your central command center is your head, to the detriment of spiritual needs, you trigger an insuppressible avalanche of thoughts. In this field, the mind is the undisputed master and has enormous capabilities when it comes to deceiving and leading us astray. It is able to "anticipate the future", conjure up delusive visions of some sort of beautiful utopia or of dreams fulfilled. It repeats to us that "just a little longer and it'll come true", even though this will never be the case! This is why it is better to be guided by the heart, because the heart is the emotions center, thanks to which you feel. You are closer to yourself. When you feel, you are more conscious and integrated. When you feel, there is a greater chance that something good will happen in your life. Don't try to fight with your thoughts, for this will only generate more of them, and the mind is unsurpassed in this. Instead of battling your thoughts, concentrate on tuning into and trusting your intuition. Don't preoccupy yourself with what to do in order to be happy. Whatever you do, do it with your heart. If you use your mind to seek happiness, you are bound to fail. There is nothing in the world that can bring you happiness unless you discover anew, just as a child would, the happiness inside you. The pursuit of happiness is a misapprehension. By searching for it, you will never find it, for this happiness is in your heart. You don't need to do anything other than agree to be happy. We were born to be happy. Every day you wake up and have received a present – the possibility of experiencing another day's happiness, You are the one who decides how much time from that day of happiness you wish to give away voluntarily to focus on something unpleasant that robs you of this joy. You could devote your time to something that brings you pleasure, or choose to listen to negative messages, and engage in gloomy, destructive conversation.

Your favorite vase, the one with such sentimental value, has got smashed. You can either spend the whole day in despair or consciously get over it. What's done is done, and there's nothing you can do to turn back time or change things back to how they were. It makes no difference whether something happened a second ago or a year ago. The past is still the past, and you can't change anything in it. You can only choose to pile on more sadness or accept it. Nobody has a duty to be happy – the choice is yours and yours alone.

Yesterday should not take time away from today.

In order to feel secure, humans need justifications, explanations and an understanding of almost everything. Since we are unable to comprehend everything, we have many questions we need an answer to. It's of no importance whether the answer is right or not. Our unconscious mind will still go through its thought and interpretation processes to confirm its own preconceived assumptions. On the basis of false or fictitious information it draws conclusions that become the solid foundations of the reasoning that follows. As it is most difficult to imagine how things could be different, many people, utterly unconsciously, do not wish to learn the truth. They unwittingly search for confirmation of what they believe or assume. The unconscious mind works in a very simple way. It assumes that others think the way we do, that everyone perceives life the same way we do; it judges others according to the criteria we employ. This is why we unwittingly make assumptions about what others think, and then we believe resolutely in it. This hidden mechanism is also the main reason why we are afraid to be ourselves among other people, why we behave as we think others expect or require. This is because we unconsciously think that others can judge us, hurt us, or blame us in the same way that we do to others.

Even if we are not sure about something in relation to another person, we make assumptions very quickly and unconsciously, simply because we lack the courage to ask them. In this way, the mind satisfies its need for information. We start from the assumption that others should know our wants and expectations. These assumptions become our sole truth, which we are prepared to defend even at the cost of breaking off relationships or contacts. We unconsciously assume that asking questions might be hazardous, as we might hear a truth we really don't want to hear. What's more, we are very often convinced that our perception of reality is the only correct one. If someone sees it differently, it means that they are wrong. Any attempt to undermine our beliefs or rightfulness will trigger our ego's defense mechanism. We are able to defend it even at the price of a relationship or great friendship destroyed. We are utterly convinced of the correctness of our knowledge, but we have neither the courage nor the willingness to test the veracity of the sources of that knowledge.

***

Parable / Metaphor:

A person is sitting on a rock, pondering: "I've got another difficult day ahead of me tomorrow. The children will be naughty, the neighbor will start picking fights. I keep meeting unpleasant people. Nothing seems to work out for me".

God (however you understand it) listens to all this and thinks to himself: "Strange wishes they may be, but, well, I must make them come true."

***

The mind's inclination to make assumptions also results in a tendency to apply labels to others. If we make assumptions about another in advance, or are attached to an opinion about that person, we are not truly interested in the person they really are. We only care about our opinion about him or her. No matter what they do or say, the mind will enter into a thought process that interprets and reasons in a way that confirms our preconceived assumptions. This is a kind of blindness and mental laziness. In the case of a negative label, we automatically generate large quantities of emotional poison in ourselves. We interpret all ambiguities as a trick and take any words said to heart. Since we are afraid to ask directly to clarify the situation, we make negative assumptions about the other person. If we come across another person who is susceptible to negative conversations, we start to gossip, automatically transmitting more and more poison and negativity. Such a conversation comes down to defending negative assumptions about a person. In this way, we paint a very negative picture of this 'guilty' person in our mind, just because we didn't have the courage to ask or to clarify a question that was unclear or incomprehensible. If you want to humiliate someone, you must first increase their guilt decisively.

Hostility disappears immediately if
one of the parties renounces it.

It's not important whether the labels we apply are positive or negative. When we meet somebody again after a long absence, or when we've heard something about them, we regard them in the light of the opinions we have about them, even though this person might have changed a lot in the meantime. For positive labels we place a halo over this person. We trust them implicitly and believe everything they say. Often, blinded by these beautiful imaginings, we completely let down our mind's guard, which leaves us defenseless if we come across somebody inclined to take advantage of this to manipulate us in any way possible or to deceive and cheat us in something. It is unfortunately the case that only those we trust are capable of doing this, while those we do not trust have no chance whatsoever.

> We are ready to believe anything,
> but not to learn the truth.

Many conflicts and problems between people will not arise if we teach ourselves to communicate in a way that is undeniably simpler and clearer, if we become more conscious in our communication with others.

If you don't understand something or are unsure, it is always better to ask than surmise and assume from the outset, as such assumptions lead to the greatest misunderstandings, whose origins lie not in reality but in our imagination. It is most often the case that it is not somebody's words or deeds that harm us, but our how we misinterpret them, which we then blindly defend. As time passes, we harbor a dislike of that person within us, though we ourselves are still not sure why.

Don't be afraid to ask when you are unsure or have doubts. Don't be afraid to say "yes", don't be scared of saying "no", and your life will change completely, for your relations with others will change. They will become clearer, more understandable and true, free of the emotional poison generated by fallacious assumptions and interpretations. By expressing your thoughts in a kind, clear and simple way, and without assuming a hostile or defensive stance, you avoid many misunderstandings stemming from false presumptions and assumptions.

We very often carry a great deal of stress within ourselves due to various problems that we are unaware of or are unable to deal with. When this stress reaches its culmination, the unconscious mind uses any pretext to unload it onto those closest to us. We need a random victim to free ourselves from tensions we are no longer able to bottle up. It will always be the person closest to our heart for, after all, we don't express our feelings to just anyone. Releasing tension does not always take an aggressive form. It often manifests itself in the form of criticism or admonishment. For example, when you criticize someone close to you, you justify it as being for their good, so they can learn from it. It's just a typical trick of the mind. Look deeper. You were angry and you wanted to unload it on someone. You couldn't be mad at your superior, a partner you depend on, and so on. You needed a random victim. By criticizing someone, we make that person feel worse, take their energy from them, and so we feel better for a while. This is because we have taken a little energy from the person closest to us, and, in line with principle of balance in the Universe, this means that in other circumstances we will find ourselves in a similar situation and everything will start to repeat. A vicious circle is formed. Such behavior merely discharges the tension temporarily, because the problem has not been solved in a conscious way. Unconscious stress relief always hurts those close to us, the innocent victims who suffered simply because they were closest. This relieves us of internal tension, but only on the surface and just briefly. In actual fact, no problem has been resolved, and the stress will return with double the intensity, compounded by an unconscious sense of guilt for hurting those closest to us. Therefore, always try to discover the real reason for your behavior, otherwise your mind will lie to you each time and keep you believing that the reason lay somewhere else. Your mind lies to you constantly. If you are aware of the real reasons for your behavior, the mind will become increasingly incapable of manipulating you. Being aware of your own reactions will allow you to start discharging your stress in a conscious way, without having to hurt those close to your heart. When you become aware of the true reasons for how you behave, a great transformation process will begin inside you, your energy polarity will change, you will start to attract more and more positive energy. Your energy will start to vibrate in an unimpeded way, resonating with the abundant energy of the Universe, which it is ready to share with you.

**

You always need to find the courage to battle against the fear of discovering the truth.

Do not fear death. Fear of dying is the first and most important source of negative energy. All other fears grow out of these beginnings. An exaggerated fear of death restrains us from experiencing the full joy of life.

Only a full acceptance of the consciousness that death is only the quintessence of existence allows you to experience life to the full. Whilever we flee from this objective truth, we will not live a full life, and the thought of death subconsciously paralyzes all our actions. As time passes, the consciousness of death will imbue our lives with ever greater frustration, regret, and a sense of everything slipping away. Our whole life will begin to oscillate around the loss of the subconscious fight against passing time and our attempt to stop it. This struggle will dominate our life, taking up all the time that could be spent on the joy of living. Paradoxically, it is only the acceptance of death and passing that allows one to fully enjoy life and affirm it.

Don't torment yourself with thoughts of sudden and solemn partings. Constantly worrying about losing your loved ones prevents or even paralyzes you from taking a step forward. If there is no way or means to bring them back to life, you should leave them in peace. In the past.

You have to say goodbye to the past, not because it is bad, but because it is already dead.

***

It's not the world or the others around you that make you happy or unhappy. It's your thoughts that do this. Nobody other than you yourself can make you happy, just as nobody can make you unhappy, unless you decide to let it happen. And if you do, then the whole world around you will help you get stuck in this unhappiness.

***

No one can harm us
as greatly as we can harm
ourselves with our
own thoughts.

***

Be the person you are.
Never try to be somebody you are not,
and you will become free. Freedom means
accepting the price of being yourself,
irrespective of how high a price it is.

***

FREEDOM AND RESPONSIBILITY

Nobody has responsibility for your life other than you, yourself. Only once you understand this, will you be able to change anything. Your mind will always put the blame on somebody else, will search for thousands of reasons to be able to externalize responsibility. It will find numerous justifications and reasons to evade responsibility. It is always somebody else who makes you suffer: your partner, your friends, your children, the social, the political, the economic system etc. An endless number of justifications and reasons can always be found in order to be able to shirk responsibility for your own life. If you tell yourself that you can't do or achieve anything, or that you suffer for reasons outside your influence, which are beyond your control, then there is nothing you can do to change this situation, because the problem lies outside. But the truth is that all the justifications and excuses serve only one purpose and that is to avoid looking into yourself, to escape responsibility for your life.

To feel better, we usually want someone else to change for us. We think, "I feel good because others are alright." Unfortunately, it doesn't work that way, it's the wrong line of thinking.

Everything around you will be in harmony
with you on condition that you are
in harmony with yourself.

Do not try to change others or the reality around you. Many have wanted to change the world before, but somehow nobody succeeded, and from what I've read, it did not end well for them. If you want to change the world, set an example yourself, but never tell it how to change.

If you limit yourself to changing only the outside world, if you only change everything around you, start a new job, meet new people, change your home and surroundings, such changes will never change you. But if you change yourself, then the world will change too - there will be one more extra person in this world who has changed. Therefore, work on yourself, not on others. Do it solely for yourself, without looking for any great philosophy or limitations.

The only way to change yourself is through rejecting the ways of reasoning you've followed so far. The greatest change doesn't come from discovering new lands, but through looking at old ones in a new way.

***

Negative feelings live within you, not in the reality around you. So don't waste your energy trying to change it - it's crazy. Don't try to change others - you stand no chance, it's simply a waste of time. Negative feelings are within you. Nobody else in the whole world can make you happy, if you can't find happiness in yourself. If you are unhappy, it is you who are unhappy. There is nobody else forcing you to feel that way. If you get angry, it is you who gets angry. No one can make you feel angry unless you decide to do it. Just like nobody but you yourself can hurt you, unless you let them. It is often the case that it is not somebody else's words that harm us, but our wrong interpretation of what they mean. And most of the time, we need another person simply to be able to transfer responsibility onto them.

More often than not we feel very bad or see ourselves as a victim when the circumstances do not meet our expectations.

There are so many people who are convinced that their role in today's world is that of a victim: abused, defenseless and innocent. They live in constant fear, an unabating feeling of threat, suffering from a lack of trust in the world and people around them. The main reason for such an attitude is that they lack self-confidence and don't trust themselves. Such people are constantly searching for authority figures they could trust, they yearn for external support or anything that could give them faith. But this is the wrong approach and will not bring any changes in life, for in order to be able to trust anyone or believe in anything, you first have to trust and believe in yourself. Rediscover the child-like trust you were born with. There is no need to search for external sources of faith and trust. Take responsibility for your own life, believe in yourself, trust yourself, and then instead of defenselessness, you will enjoy great strength, and instead of fear, you will be filled with courage.

Primal reality rests within your inner self. External reality is merely its reflection. This means there is always a reason for whatever happens to us. If succeed in finding this reality within yourself and take responsibility for it, you will free yourself from suffering and will gain wisdom. Every lesson we experience in life is there to teach us something. And this goes for every single detail. Nothing, absolutely nothing happens by chance. Everything that happens to us is to teach us something, foster our development, make us stronger and help us move onwards, even when our mind and ego refuse to accept it.

Only once we identify the source of our painful experiences can we free ourselves from them without the need to live through them again and again. Therefore, it is essential to keep an eye on all of our imagination, our desires and resentments, the feelings they trigger when you experience them and after you actually fulfill them. We gain wisdom through understanding them, not through fighting or suppressing them.

This might seem hard, because it requires courage and responsibility for your own life, for your own choices and actions. It requires taking responsibility for what you have done, but also for what you haven't, or what you have neglected. You can always resort to some kind of philosophy that will help you justify your lack of courage. But if you do lack courage, don't blame others for that. Do not blame yourself, either, because the feeling of guilt is a very bad and destructive feeling. Avoid it just as you would the devil himself. When you feel guilty, not only do you hate the mistakes you've made, but you also hate yourself. It's enough to be aware of this and take responsibility for it. Hell is not a situation or another person – it's your thoughts.

You can't hold anybody accountable for your own happiness, for your own life, your own development, for the development of your own awareness. The degree of responsibility you are ready to take for your own life determines how many changes you are able to make during it.

> Someone who does not trust themselves
> will never be able to trust another.

If you have enough courage to look deep inside yourself, you will notice how vast the vacuum is that you try to fill with other people. But at the same time, you feel they suffocate you. These are the ones who control your behavior and emotions. With their presence they mitigate your feeling of loneliness. They lift your spirits with their appreciation, praise and acceptance, while at the same time making you feel sad, causing you pain and depressing you with their criticism or disapproval. Just stop and think: How often do you follow norms, principles and rules foisted on you by others? You seek their company, crave their love, fear their rejection, yearn for their acclaim, you humbly yield to the imposed pangs of conscience. Others know better what is good and what is bad for you. Even the mere thought that it might be possible to act differently, against the imposed norms, mindset and behavior, has a paralyzing effect. The only way to free yourself from this kind of enslavement and dependence is to be aware of this situation. A free and self-aware person will never agree to remain in this kind of dependence all their life.

Do not let others control over your own life. Don't let others manipulate the way you feel. Don't use excuses like: "I'm stressed because of you", "This person drives me crazy", "They told me to do so", "You always hold me back", "It's all your fault". Take away from "them" the right to influence your emotions and decide about your life. You aren't now and will never be able to determine what others do or how they act. It is only you, though, who can influence your own reactions and behavior. Do not worry about what others say and do. Everyone has the right to speak and do what they think is right for them, and you are not obliged to react to all this. If someone keeps telling you that you are going to go wrong or that you won't manage do something, don't get carried away by your emotions and don't let someone else's words set limits to what you can do. Bear in mind that this person is talking about their own limitations, not yours. Don't worry if someone claims you are different. Just consider how many people there are in the world who are the same. Don't let mediocrity enslave you. Don't pass responsibility on to other people or circumstances - take full responsibility for your own life and you will grow. Your life will become more peaceful and more self-aware.

We very often let others interfere with our lives; we accept it and act according to the norms and rules imposed by others, because unconsciously we fear that if we don't do so, we will become lonely and we will be deprived of love.

Do not let the fear of rejection and loneliness paralyze you, limit your development and your way towards freedom.

> You don't knock on all the closed doors and
> don't go into all that are open.

Nowadays, more and more people are searching for the path of their own development and are interested in spirituality. Books on this subject take up ever more shelf space in book stores. Once you set out on the path of spiritual development, you will always follow this track. Just like someone sitting in a dark cave who spots a chink of light in the distance and heads off towards it. However, you have to remember that you will have to walk some of life's paths on your own. When you develop, you become more self-aware, and this way more alone, but you shouldn't confuse it with loneliness. Loneliness is a feeling that grips you when you keep escaping loneliness, when you fear that you are not ready to accept it. Being consciously alone is the beautiful feeling of being alone with yourself, but not lonely. If you fear loneliness and you can't accept it, this is when you start feeling lonely. And then you are ready to do anything, even go against your best interests, simply to please others. You will always be able to find a crowd, some kind of mind-altering substance or psychotropic drug that will help you forget yourself. Loneliness will shape its own magic oblivion.

Accept being on your own, accept your ability to spend time alone with yourself, and then you will see that you are never lonely.

***

Parable / Metaphor:

Around nine o'clock in the morning, a man came to a carpenter's workshop. He inquired if there would be any work for him. The carpenter asked how much he wanted for the job from nine o'clock in the morning until sunset. The man replied that $50 would do, which the carpenter agreed to and the man was happy to take up the job. Around noon, another man came to the same workshop and asked about being taken on. The carpenter asked how much he would like to be paid for the work from noon to sunset. The man replied that $50 would do, which the carpenter agreed to, and the man was happy to take up the job. On the same day in the afternoon, about three o'clock, yet another man came to the workshop with the same question. The carpenter also asked what amount of money he would like to be paid for his work from three o'clock to sunset. The man replied that $50 would do, which the carpenter agreed to. At the end of the day, after sunset, everyone got together and each man got the money they had agreed to. Two men got very upset and started to protest that it was unfair and that they felt cheated. The carpenter calmly answered them: "I did not cheat you. Why are you protesting and why are you dissatisfied? Didn't I pay you exactly what you had asked for?"

***

By complaining, you automatically adopt the role of a victim. Don't feel pity yourself or find comfort in complaining. There will always be someone better, and someone who is worse off than you. Thinking about the unwanted keeps you tied to the past, and blocks the future.

Frustration and complaining are always reflect a lack of acceptance of the here and now. They carry a heavy load of negative energy. Once you start thinking or acting sensible in a particular situation, you take matters into our hands. Instead of complaining, you move into action, if this is necessary or possible. The other options you have are either to leave the scheme or accept it. In every situation we have three options. Change the circumstances that take your joy away from you. If you can't change them, you can simply walk away from them. If you can neither change them nor walk away from them, you have to accept them, and this will also bring peace to your heart. If you don't want to do anything about the situation, and you are stuck in it, this means that you have in fact grown to like your discontent, that you have identified yourself with it so much that you can no longer live without it. Your discontent has become part of your own identity, it's your free choice and no one is to blame for it.

Only few people can lead a truly happy life. A fair share of the population unconsciously love to feel bad. They sleepwalk through life along corridors marked out by the walls of their own dogmas, yet never trying to change them. They walk on like the blind, not entertaining the thought that there might be another way, that it is possible to live differently. They are in fact almost happy, while being unhappy, because there are very few who can imagine or have an idea of what they could do if they became happy. They voluntarily nurture their sadness and dissatisfaction. By constantly creating negative visions, they lock themselves in the shackles of their own misery. Nobody forces them to do so nor keeps them in this situation by force. Unfortunately, such people put the blame wholly on others and reject even the slightest notion of being accountable for the situation. They're notoriously resentful and put the blame on others. "I'm unhappy because of the people around me. They cause me pain and it is their fault that I can't be happy". This is a typical trick of the mind. Everybody else is to blame except for me. Unfortunately, unhappy people do not even allow themselves to take responsibility for this.

This kind of mindset is the reason why nothing can change in our life, because by shifting the blame away from us, to the outside, we subconsciously release ourselves from the burden of taking responsibility for any change. "Since the cause lies outside, it is beyond me, then, poor me, what can I do? Nothing, I have to remain stuck in my misery".

Take a look around you and you'll see that there are so many people who are lazy, almost covered in dust, sluggish, devoid of any vitality or willingness to live, averse to any change, paralyzed by the mere thought of taking responsibility for their own lives.

Never speak badly about yourself.

The human mind works in a very simple way. Sadness always comes when external circumstances have not adapted to the mind's expectations. Once you understand the way your mind works and you take responsibility for your sadness, something will start to change in your life and you will slowly extricate yourself from the rut of misery.

A person who is mature and self-aware is also responsible for their own choices or their inability to make a decision. Only slaves are deprived of the right to choose, condemned by their masters to enslavement. A free person always has a choice. The greatest evil is to complain without any tangible attempt to change the existing situation. Once you understand how this process works, happiness will begin to follow you, like your shadow.

Nobody is born to be unhappy. Every new-born child is destined to be happy. It takes huge courage to rid yourself of fear and live up to your destiny. Only when you accept full responsibility for yourself, for who you are, will you become mature. This is the door to happiness and the greatest courage. But most people are afraid to accept it, they fear this responsibility. For fear of accepting responsibility for our own lives, we tell ourselves that others are responsible. "Poor, me, what can I do? I am helpless, because others stand in my way, they hinder and restrain me, they tie my hands. All I can do is grieve or mourn my fate." How often do you tell yourself that you can't do something because others restrict you or the situation you are in doesn't allow it? It's very convenient: no burdens, no feelings of guilt. In this sense, slavery becomes your freedom, freedom from responsibility and from a conscious free choice. If you act this way, everything gets worse. And then you sink deeper and deeper, becoming even more unhappy.

Don't let fear take over your mind and take control of your life. Tell yourself, "I am responsible for my own life, for everything that has happened to me. This is the fruit of the seeds I sowed earlier, and now is the time to reap it. I can't turn back the clock: whatever has happened, has happened. Every thought I make, every decision I take is a step in the direction of my future.

If you look deep into yourself, your life will enter a new dimension, bringing a revolutionary change in your consciousness. Everything will begin to change, because you will become aware that you are responsible for your life. You and only you.

Even if you think that circumstances restrict you, you can still live a life of happiness. The situation you find yourself in or the people around you may force you to behave in a particular way, but they can never force you to think in a particular way. The spirit in an enslaved body is always free. You can either sit in despair over your fate or steadfastly persevere. If you want to live, you must move forward. Even when your feet are chained, you can still walk, sing and dance.

In this way you overcome not only the obstacles, but also yourself.

You have no impact on many external circumstances, but you do have an impact on your thoughts, on the way you see them and how you react to them. Every decision you make determines your development. The more conscious your choices are, the more self-aware and comprehensive your development will be. This is your own choice. This is your own life.

The path you are following draws from the past, but at the same time, it paves the way to the future.

Do not let cultural circumstances or your negative experiences hold you captive. Do not let them determine your reactions and emotions.

If someone has had a bad experience with a person from a different culture, or has been bitten by a dog or got food-poisoned in a roadside bar, should they feel the negative impact of these events for the rest of their lives? Should they avoid meeting people from different cultures, fear dogs or avoid eating in roadside bars for the rest of their life?

Don't burden yourself with all your past unpleasant experiences. Shed this baggage. If you brood over these past negative experiences, you cause them to grow within you and taking away all the joy. Having to carry such a burden, you lack the strength to enjoy life. Memories make you look ahead into the future through the fog of the past. This could obscure even the clearest, undisturbed, beautiful view. The image you see is not pure: it is distorted by your memories.

The way you perceive the world, your attitude and approach towards it, is your world. If you want to change your world, change the way you look at and your mindset. Whatever has happened is now in the past, and the past is something you can't change at all. It's time to move on. Our experiences make us wiser – they are what is worth taking from the past. Learn to enjoy every new moment, uncontaminated by memories.

> Occupying yourself with unpleasant things
> reduces your ability to find joy.

As children, when we did something wrong, most of the time parents, older siblings, tutors or teachers would be there to scold us. In such situations, we felt bad or very ashamed. If such situations happen quite often in a child's life, the child, completely unconsciously and unwittingly, starts to hesitate before trying something new. From the point of view of such a child, restraining themself from making decisions or even harboring an aversion towards any new challenges seems to be the wisest and most reasonable choice.

Unfortunately, such an attitude becomes deeply rooted in the child's subconscious and is then transferred to his or her adult life. That is why, whenever faced with any new challenges or experiences, we unconsciously prefer to be stuck with what we know, because it is "what's familiar". Anything that is unknown triggers fear, reluctance or worries. Even if the circumstances we have found ourselves in for years are not favorable to us, or even when we don't want them, a subconscious fear of taking up any new challenges unconsciously locks us into the old, for this is at least something familiar.

This deeply rooted, unconscious fear of the new, of any change, keeps us stuck, as if we were paralyzed, in something that we don't want or even hate and don't accept.

The lack of courage to look at the situation more deeply makes the mind start its games. When faced with important decisions, it most often suggests thoughts like: I'll think about it later, I'll do it later, I'll make myself a coffee now, clean up, read, etc. This way, you can waste your whole life on irrelevant, sometimes meaningless things. How often we waste our time on things we won't even remember tomorrow, just to postpone the moment of making a decision in life. On top of that, we can also waste time on reminiscing or making plans, forgetting that life is going on here and now, and not in the past or the future. All these tricks of the mind serve only one purpose - to escape the responsibility for your own life.

Running away from ourselves, out of fear of being confronted with the real cause of our negative emotions, we create a void deep within ourselves, which we try to fill with various 'substances'. These might be meaningless, hollow social encounters, compulsive shopping, sex, gambling, medication, workaholism, alcohol or drugs. Unfortunately, this kind of escape does not change anything and does not heal our negative emotions. On the contrary, over time, dissatisfaction, frustration or the feeling of a meaningless life start to build up rapidly, leading to a need for even more of such fillers.

The mind is capable of inventing thousands of completely irrelevant reasons for postponing important decisions in life, for putting off changes almost indefinitely, and delaying the moment for taking any risk whatsoever.

If you're unhappy and want to change something in your life, you need to take resolute action, instead of running away from it and put it off endlessly. The ability to close a certain chapter in your life with dignity is a sign of great wisdom; let go of what was in the past and liberate yourself. Not out of arrogance, pride or weakness, but in order to make room for something new. There is no more room for the things of the past. Close the door behind what was there before, and open it to what is yet to come, to something new.

It's always better to do anything at all than nothing, especially if you have been stuck in a strange and unhappy situation. Act slowly, but act. The biggest weakness is to give up and do nothing. Failure is acceptable, but not idleness. Even if you make a mistake, you will at least learn something, so ultimately it won't turn out to be such a big mistake or failure. Every failure contains the seed of equivalent or even greater benefit, so looks for the positive in everything that has happened, and you will continue to thrive. But if, instead, you constantly remain stuck in the same situation, you will never learn anything. It is usually fear that stops you from trying to take any action. Stand in front of the mirror, look yourself in the eye and be brave enough to admit to yourself that you don't have sufficient courage, that you are afraid of taking responsibility for your own life, and that is why you saddle others with the blame.

The source of all your dilemmas, fears and anxieties can only be found within yourself. And it is only there that you can find the source of power to overcome them. Be a self-aware observer of your own fears and anxieties, and only this way will you manage to break the connection between your fears and your way of thinking. If it is the fear of failure that paralyzes you and makes literally any action impossible, then remember that failure is in fact not the worst that can happen to you. The greatest evil lies in not trying at all, and just being stuck in a situation that continually destroys and kills you, day by day, piece by piece.

Nobody can provide you with instructions and guidelines that you could follow to lead a happy life. Nobody can mark out the path your life will take and tell you how to live, no matter how great, wonderful or saintly this person is. The moment you try to emulate somebody or become like them, you start betraying who you really are. Think of the uniqueness that you carry within you. Even the most wonderful of others' paths through life are theirs, and this doesn't mean that you will be able to feel happiness and fulfillment when following these paths. This is because every person is unique, one-of-the-kind. If you follow somebody else's path, you lose the sense of your own worth, because subconsciously you will continue to carry the burden of having no courage to follow your own unique route. Nobody is born to walk the paths set by others, just as nobody is born to fulfill other people's expectations of what they should be like. Sometimes when you say "Yes" to others, you may at the same time be saying "No" to yourself.

Our mind is on a constant quest for explanation and answers. It is not capable of moving on without a map or guide. Therefore sometimes we can expect others to share a good piece of advice, sometimes they can help us find the right direction, but this is all, nothing more than that. It's because life is a great mystery. Leading a true life means living with a sense of mystery that you cannot explain without experiencing it yourself.

Traveling through life, you have to discover and blaze your own trail, tread your own paths that are compatible with who you are inside, paths that follow your heart. Even the most beautiful of maps that belongs to somebody else will not match your life. You can't blindly follow the paths trodden by others, even when they seem straighter and easier, because that way you will never achieve happiness and fulfillment. Sometimes you'll find yourself at a crossroads, or you might lose your way; you might also fall, but getting lost and falling down are an integral part of life.

It's only natural to fall down, doubt, get back up and continue your journey through life. Don't worry and don't blame yourself for this. This is what makes you develop and gain strength, no matter how many times you stumble and fall while on the road. It's not the fall that destroys you, it's when you don't get up. That's why every time you just have to get up, just shake yourself off and move on. Every time you get up, you become stronger. This is the only way to achieve true power and fulfillment.

The greatest reason to be proud doesn't come from the fact that you never fall, but that whenever you fall, you pick yourself back up again.

There will be a few obstacles on your way, but when you encounter them, make sure you don't become one of them. It might also happen on many occasions that you get caught by the dark, get completely lost, lose your bearings and the sense of which direction to go in. You will feel helpless and you will be in need of some guidance and direction signs, but ultimately you are the one to decide which way to go. If it is important for you to live a happy life, you will certainly find the right way. To succeed in life you must not only act, but also dream, not only plan, but also believe. If your plan doesn't work, change the plan, but never your aim.

> Don't look where you landed,
> but what you tripped on.

Life is beautiful, because it allows us to discover its mysteries. But only those who have the courage to follow their own heart will be able to do this. It is only by following your own path, by blazing your own trails, that you will feel truly alive. Only then will you achieve fulfillment. Your life will fill with happiness and joy, and only then will you be able to reach your destination.

Life is not made up of some great, wonderful matters. Life is a myriad of small things - meetings with family, friends, walks without any specific destination, preparing a meal, washing, cleaning, watering the plants. If you focus only on the 'big things', you will miss out on life. The way you treat all these little things shows how much respect you have for life. Respect these little things and be aware of them. Out of respect for the small things in life grows respect for your own life and that of others around you. Aim to devote as much of your time as possible to activities that you love and enjoy, those that absorb you completely. Do not succumb to pressure from others when they try to convince you that what you are doing is useless, worthless, a mere waste of time. Regardless of their usefulness, keep doing those things out of the sheer joy that they bring you. Put all your heart into them, all the commitment you can afford. Put as much attention into them as you can, and then they will become your gateway to love and freedom. Do not let others hinder you in doing the things you love. Don't let someone else control your joy, so that you don't fall into the trap of control and dependence on other people.

All the things you do with love, just for the sheer joy of doing them, make up the right and only way towards freedom and independence. When doing these things, you fill up with love, whose glow will then radiate from you onto the whole world of people and things around you.

The path to freedom does not lead through other people's views and opinions, but through your daily activities. Therefore, whatever you do, put all your heart into it and all the commitment you can afford. Everything you do without being conviction brings only misfortune, dissatisfaction, anxiety, pain and tension, because every time you act without commitment and enthusiasm, you divide yourself into two parts. One part of you does something and the other opposes it. You engage only one part of the self, while the other part resists, rebels and fights. This is one of the greatest misfortunes that can happen to you. This is because tear yourself inside.

Have a strong self of your worth and believe in what you do. It makes no difference what you do, the activities you get involved or whether you are fully committed to them. If you are divided within yourself, your actions will always result in dissatisfaction. Being fully committed to what you are doing will bring you joy. When performed with complete commitment, even the most mundane everyday activities can bring satisfaction and a feeling of fulfillment that will make you radiate from within. Everything you do without fervor, whatever it may be, will give you no satisfaction. Living life in a half-hearted way without being fully committed, will create your own internal hell, which will grow from one moment to the next.

Your time on Earth is limited. Don't waste it by dealing with somebody else's life, nor by battling with things or circumstances which you cannot influence. Don't try to be someone else, and don't live other people's lives. Be yourself. No one was born to live the way others want or require. Do not close your life within the walls of your own dogmas. Do not try to live according to other's opinions simply to meet their expectations. Do not let others' opinions drown out your inner voice. Be courageous enough to follow your heart and intuition. Love people and be yourself.

Better to be one of the few than of one of the many. Overcome the view that you have to be average. Grasp life with your hands. Follow the voice of your heart. If you learn to listen to yourself, you will go astray, and there will come a time in your life when you are far from problems and the people who create them. You will start to surround yourself with people you can laugh with. You will forget about the bad things and focus on the good. Sometimes you will fall, but such falls are part and parcel of life and it is through them that you develop. You will begin to enjoy the fleeting pleasures of real life around you, because you have lost your fear of missing them. You will stop clinging tight to them, and so you'll take pleasure in experiencing them. You will appreciate all sensual pleasures, but they will not become your goal. By enjoying them, you will nourish your inner sensations instead of inflating your ego. You will stop being attached to this world at the level of observable reality. You will feel a connection with the whole Universe. You will experience contact with something much, much bigger. You won't need the world in any way other than as it really is.

Feelings of guilt mean you lose the joy of life. How can you enjoy life if you carry feelings of guilt inside? I did bad there, and there etc. - such feelings of guilt can destroy your entire life. How is it possible to live joyfully with that baggage? Enjoying life just doesn't seem possible. You become heavy, overwhelmed, walking dead.

Guilty feelings destroy those who bottle them up. Whatever's done cannot be undone. You can't change the past. You must understand the essence of your mistakes and not repeat them. You and only you can forgive yourself for past mistakes. Remember: as we develop, our awareness grows, we know more and understand more, and, as a result, we act differently. You cannot judge your past behavior through the prism of your present state of consciousness. This is a sin above all others, one that kills the joy of life, crushes you like a rock. How can you love, live, sing and dance with such a burden?

> Don't allow your past
> to become your limitation.

Accept life the way it is. To strike the right balance, just take life as it comes. Life is not something to be chosen, but rather something to experience. Stress, distress and fears are normal elements of existence. Accepting the toughest aspects of life will make you stronger and more resilient. A single moment in which you accept the reality around you is so much better than years of stress, revolt and struggle. If you stop rebelling, forgive yourself for past mistakes, and also discount others' imperfections and do this with love, then you will become free. Freedom is your inner nature – you were born with it. Don't let the past, over which you have no influence, burden and restrain you. Don't live your life with a feeling of regret. You can't change the past. There is a reason for everything that happens and even bad events can teach us something. In fact, they are essential on the road to progress. Blaming yourself for things you didn't do will also prove fruitless. Forgive yourself and forget past mistakes, then you will regain happiness and the joy of life.

Most of us spend our lives thinking about the past or future. Wrapped up in our beautiful visions of the future, how often do we view the present as merely being the vehicle that will transport us into it. Our thoughts very rarely impinge on reality. This only happens in moments of sudden beauty or danger, in a meeting with a loved one or a surprise at the unexpected.

Just consider how much of your life is spent waiting for what you've imagined to be the perfect moment to arrive. Some people spend their whole life waiting to be able to live their life.

Waiting is a state of mind based on desiring the future while pushing away the present. You reject what you have and desire what you don't have. The future becomes an abstract concept in order to escape from reality. You become the architect of your own life, who wishes to construct a beautiful building while completely neglecting the foundations.

That's how internal splits and stress are generated. They manifest themselves when you are "here", but you would rather be "there", or when you are in the present but want to move yourself into the future. You become irritated that the great future or situation you have created for yourself hasn't happened yet, and that you have to wait for it. If you can't find pleasure and peace in the here and now, the future will drift by alongside you like a cloud, unnoticed. You won't be able to experience it when it becomes the present, because your mind is imprisoned in memories and expectations.

Happiness, joy and peace are only possible here and now, at the present time. If you cannot find them now, you are certain not to find them in the future or the past. If you are tied to the past or allow yourself to be trapped by expectations, life will slip away unnoticed.

There are few who are able to live consciously and mindfully in the present. With goals and plans and absorbed in the future, we stumble on the stones that lie in our path. Our thoughts are focused on our future goal, entirely eliminating the present.

Don't be afraid to pursue your dreams, but if you have singled out a particular goal or plan, move in that direction without concentrating on it, just go towards it. If you keep in mind the goal you want to reach, and start to pay greater attention to each step, you will find solutions to some problems before they arise. If you desire something, don't be impatient, for it's a question of more haste, less speed. When you want something, wait patiently and calmly. You have sowed seed that is germinating and will grow, but there is no way you can speed this process up.

Everything requires time. Work is necessary, but leave the rest to God (however you understand this). Impatience rears its head at times, but it appears together with desire, which creates an obstacle. Retain the desire but reject the impatience, because it generates stress and delays. Don't confuse impatience with desire. Desire contains longing, but no fight. Impatience has fight but no longing. Longing includes waiting, but no demands, while impatience has demands but no waiting. Desiring is natural positive energy, impatience is stress and negative energy. The Universe always responds with the same kind of energy you generate. Each and every negative thought, even the most secret one, will hit you back with great force.

Do everything with great faith, conviction and complete commitment. Don't safeguard yourself by constructing plan B's, because they prove that you don't believe what you do will succeed. Our consciousness has the power to do things and the Universe supports it with all its power. However, it must be in a state of supreme balance between ideas, beliefs, and convictions. Without faith and conviction even the greatest ideas will be rejected.

If you take every step with an awareness of the goal and with complete mindfulness, faith and conviction, you are sure to reach this goal very swiftly. A lack of mindfulness and consciousness at the present time will cause you to trip over everything that lies in your way. It's highly likely that with this lack of consciousness at this moment, you will stumble over the obstacles in your path so hard that achieving this goal will prove impossible.

Don't pursue thoughts like a shadow follows the light. Don't chase ideas or how they are projected. Be cautious, joyful and calm in the present moment. Your life is the time and place you are in, and life goes on in the present, not in the future nor in the past. Life is a strange creation. No one knows when it started, no one knows when it will end, and it only exists in the here and now. Whatever you do, don't let the future steer your mind, don't let the past bother you, for the past no longer exists, and the future does not yet exist. You can only experience mindfulness, happiness and peace in the present. To achieve this, you do not have to be in a special place, in a very distant land.

There's a simple secret to happiness. Learn to listen to your heart. Listen in a very conscious, attentive and pure way, not distracted by the desires of the mind, by fanciful images or memories. Learn this and your life will become happy and peaceful. It will begin to follow its own path, without the need to ponder what is right and what is wrong.

How often we hide behind the notion of God, authority figures, destiny, karma, circumstances, etc., just to shed responsibility for our own lives, for our own development. The mind constantly seeks to place responsibility outside itself, away from itself. However, the degree to which you are willing to take responsibility for your own life determines how it will look and how much you can achieve in it.

If they are incapable of finding the responsibility for their own lives within themselves, very many people retreat into mind-altering substances, psychotropics, alcohol or drugs, into anything that renders the mind unaware of their own responsibility. However, this is not the answer, and it won't change anything. Many such solutions can be used right up until death, running away from the responsibility for our life. If you lack the courage, don't burden others with this.

When you understand that you and only you are responsible for your own life, you will not flee into the unconscious, but will start to tread your own path of development. This gives you enormous strength, energy, and the whole Universe supports you in this.

> Life in memory, in the imagination,
> is life that does not exist.

You wake each morning and start to paint another picture in your mind. You can choose bright or gloomy colors. You can paint sadness or joy. It all depends on what you devote your thoughts to. In your thoughts you are a completely person. The mind remains free even when the body is enslaved. This is beautiful, wonderful. You are the only one to decide what you think about and how, nobody can force you to think a particular way. You can become the glorious blooming of pure consciousness, pure beauty or a destructive, joyless, automated robot. Life is neither gray nor colorful. Life is a blank canvas, which you are given every day. It is you who decides what to paint on it and how you will express your creative invention. It is your choice, but remember:

you are responsible for it. You and only you, nobody but you.

If you want to live in happiness, live according to your inner voice. Never give up your dreams. Think like a winner and remain faithful to what is inside you. Follow your own path, the path of your heart. It is certain to be less trodden by others, but it is your road, the only one that is right for you. Do not follow the desires and aspirations of the mind. This is a very crowded road, full of hustle and bustle and danger. Live your life in harmony, because that is where the real happiness is. Happiness is within you. Everything that comes from outside is mere temporary pleasure and a springboard to "more and more". Fulfilling a desire can at most excite you and give you momentary pleasure for a moment. Do not confuse this with happiness.

Understanding this fact requires the awareness that everything depends on you. There are no excuses, no escape. You bear full responsibility and there is nobody to help you shoulder this burden. Being happy is not a matter of yesterday or tomorrow but today.

> You will never rise above what you
> don't want to look in the eye.

People devote a great deal of their time to learning how to earn a living, but don't have time for themselves to learn how to live. So what if you've learned how to make money to live if you don't know how to live? You can dedicate your whole life to thinking about making money. You can buy everything in your life: new clothes, a new car, a new house, but you can't buy back the time that has passed.

The search for paradise is the search
for the joy and trust of childhood.

We have all heard sayings such as 'Only a child can enter the heavenly kingdom', 'Until you become a child, you will not pass through the gates of paradise'. All religions speak of this. It is a beautiful metaphor, yet few really understand its meaning.

It is obvious that you your body will never again be a child's body, but your consciousness can be as pure and innocent as a child's. If you start looking at the world through a child's eyes, untainted by dogmas and prejudices, you will not know the fear of the new, and will live with a sense of a great, unsolvable mystery. At the same time, you will be a conscious observer of the reality around you, your life will become a happy one, and you will cross the boundaries of 'paradise', with no need to wait until death for this. Every one of us should discover our inner kingdom, the one we have always carried within ourselves. If you don't discover the happiness within yourself afresh, as a child would, you will never find it anywhere, not even in the most beautiful corners of the world, or fairy-tale land. We must seek out the eternal happiness that is inside us, and not content ourselves with fleeting pleasures.

The whole secret to this road is to become reborn, 'like a child'. The search for paradise is the search for the joy and trust of childhood. If you think something will be difficult for you, that you won't manage, that you can't live without your problems, dogmas and prejudices, all because they are so much a part of you, don't worry or get stressed. Please believe me when I say there's no obligation to live a happy life. It's your life and only yours. Life is a gift, but being happy is your choice.

Fate, karma, destiny, God (however you understand this), circumstances, other people, the social system – all these words belong to the same category: jettisoning responsibility for your life.

Those who are true to themselves know that deep down in their soul they have long been dissatisfied with the path they are taking, and that they would change it if only they had enough courage. Changes always generate fears, but inaction and thinking about what we don't want is nothing but a materialization and escalation of the problem. Unless you take full responsibility for your life, nothing will change in it, you will never become free, strong and independent. You won't even get a taste of freedom. You can taste this freedom, independence and strength at any time, but the price is taking full responsibility for your life.

A lot in our lives slips away and is lost forever, simply because we lack the courage to take responsibility. It is usually the case that achieving a goal does not demand a huge effort, but rather courage. Most often, it is the courage to take the first step that makes things take their own course. Even the longest journey always starts with the first step, but this is what takes the most courage. However, the very fact of taking the first step makes us feel happy, because we begin to see that our goal is actually much closer than we assumed. A little bit of courage is all it takes to feel fulfilled by taking the first step. How often the door to happiness and freedom is right next to us - all it takes is a little bit of courage to grab the handle. It doesn't take much to be unhappy. No courage or skill is needed. Anyone who escapes from life can feel that way. More often than not, all that's needed is another person or a situation we can saddle with the blame for our misfortune.

Initially, as you become more free and responsible for your life, fear and anxiety emerge, because you have to start making your own independent choices. No one is forcing or forbidding you to do anything. You have a free hand, but this is when the inner struggle between your heart and mind begins. You fear making decisions, the responsibility for them and the consequences they bring. Every decision you make is a step that marks out the direction in which your future is heading. If you make a mistake, you won't be able to blame anyone. The responsibility for your choices lies with you alone.

This is the main reason why the majority of people simply fear freedom and taking responsibility for their own life. Deep in their hearts, they would like to change something in their lives, to live in harmony with themselves, but they are paralyzed with fear at the very thought of making any kind of decision that might open the door to something new and unknown. This is why, despite being dissatisfied with their lives, they lack the courage to make any changes whatsoever, remain stuck in something they don't want, purely because it is familiar.

It takes a lot of courage to follow the road of your heart. This means living a life of love and trust, but also one with a sense of uncertainty. You have to move in the unknown, leave the past and allow your future to come true. You have to walk fearlessly on dangerous paths.

If you stop leaning on others, you will stand
on your own two feet.

The moment you cross the boundary of the unknown, your fear grows, as you feel uneasy, not knowing what you are or aren't allowed to do. You don't know what is round the corner. You are no longer sure of yourself, and you may make a mistake or lose yourself.

It is precisely this fear that binds people to whatever is familiar and which paralyzes them before making any new decisions. Somebody who is really alive will always choose the path of his or her heart, choose the unknown, take the risk despite being aware of the dangers that lie ahead. The heart is always prepared to take a gamble. The mind is afraid of risk, it calculates and calculates, it is very shrewd. The heart does not act this way. An open heart hurts no-one, a closed heart allows others to be hurt and cheated. Living in harmony with one's heart requires great courage - cowards avoid this, and in one fell swoop, become dead.

Concerns, fears, anxieties all appear, shadow-like, together with freedom and choice. Now everything begins to depend on you and only you; everything becomes your free choice. You can ask many other people for guidance and advice, but you are the one to make the final decision yourself. You and only you will be responsible for it. If you fail, you fail. If you succeed, you succeed. But it will always be your responsibility. Every choice you make becomes, in some way, a final one. You cannot turn it back, you cannot forget it, you cannot undo it or deny it. Your choice becomes your destiny. It will stay with you and be a part of you. You cannot disown it. Almost every choice is made in the dark, as nothing in life is certain. That's why somebody who is free is very often gripped by anxiety. Having to make the final decision themselves, they are plagued by questions: do this or do that?

But that is really the price of freedom.

***

If you love a flower,
do not pick it, for it will die
and stop being what you love.

Be very close but allow it to live.

Love is closeness, not possession.

***

LOVE AND RELATIONSHIPS

True love is like a mirror. The purer, nobler and more true your love, the more beautiful you see your own reflection in it.

If you want true love to come into your life, you first need to eliminate any dependence on other people. Do not treat love as a remedy for emptiness and loneliness. Stop connecting the word "love" with anybody else. You must understand that true love has no connection with any particular person. Direct your love towards the flowers, birds, trees. Just love. Touch a tree, a rock with profound love and you will see that this will not be one-sided love. Feel how you become connected, become one. Then you will feel a sudden surge of energy, you will be filled with an amazing feeling of joy and unity. You will feel joy because you express love. Whoever loves is happy and more joyful. One who cannot love is not able to feel joy. Joy is like love's shadow: it always follows it. Love everything around you and you will become happier. There is no need to worry whether this love will be reciprocated or not. Everyone has the right to love whoever they want, but not to demand reciprocity. Any love that demands to be returned is not love.

Joy follows after love, whether it is responded to or not. This is the beauty of love - it gives joy. Love is independent of what is happening outside. True love is yours and demands nothing in return. Love that expects reciprocity is not love.

Only when we gain love, respect, kindness, and
understanding for ourselves can we show
all this to others.

Whatever you do, do it with love. Involve yourself as often as possible in the things you love and do those things bring you joy and pleasure as much as possible. Be generous in love. Love the people you know and those who you don't. It is easy to love only those who love us. In time, you will begin to feel that everything is remarkable, and that the energy of love is all around you. Once you feel it, you will never again feel a lack of love, for you will receive it from the whole world. Nature will always respond to your love.

The source of true love is within you, and only when the energy of love has filled you will it be able to pour out onto others. Realize the existence of this source, which is inside you and which has always been there.

***

The authentic power of true love will only appear in you when you stop making your love dependent on other people, when you stop treating it as a remedy for loneliness. First, love yourself, fill yourself with the love you carry deep within yourself, and you will see that the world abounds in love and people overflowing with love.

***

Not loving yourself means you can't give love to another person. To forge a relationship full of love and intimacy, you first need to love and like yourself; only then can these feelings radiate outwards. If you do not love yourself, you will not be able to love anyone else. If you don't respect yourself, you won't respect other people. This is precisely why love is very often artificial and inauthentic. It has no spontaneity. If you don't respect yourself, you can't respect others. Not loving yourself means you cannot radiate love onto others. You first have to become the light for yourself, and only then will it begin to spread, filling every void, and ultimately start to radiate outwards, onto other people. You can only share with others something that you have. If you love yourself, you will share your love, if you are unhappy, you will share your misery. If you don't love yourself, why should someone else do it, why should they risk it?

Someone who doesn't love themself is unable to love anyone else. Never! The first wave of love must come from your heart. Love is about sharing with someone, but how can you share something you don't have? If you don't love yourself, what have you got that you can share? The object of first love must be oneself. Only then is another love possible. Everyone strives for this second love, knowing nothing of the first.

In traditional relationships, people live together without love, because they are incapable of loving. In such relationships, there is a lack of intimacy. Very many people live together knowing nothing of love and intimacy! They are able to live with each other for years not knowing what love and closeness are. The majority want to live together because this is more convenient, safer, but hardly any understand the nature of true love. Life is based on being together, but few know what this really means.

Love means tuning into another's feelings, closeness, conversation, taking interest in the other person and knowing their inner needs, as well as trust, warmth and care. In traditional relationships, the partners are rarely happy with each other; at most, they tolerate each other and meet each other's needs. They live with each other because they are connected by a network of different relationships or are unable or afraid to live alone. Living together is more comfortable, economical, safer and cheaper. Living alone is more difficult. It is very often the case that the wife plays many roles - the cheapest employee, housewife, cook, maid, nurse. The husband is most commonly treated as the source of financial support.

This is exactly why true love, closeness and happiness are missing from such relationships. The main reason for this is that hardly anybody is capable of loving themself. Love is an extremely rare flower that blooms only occasionally.

Many people live in the mistaken belief that they can love. They believe that they love, but this is a misconception. True love is an exceptional and unique flower that rarely comes in bloom.

A lack of respect and honesty will lead to our relationship being substandard and temporary, dominated by the fear of rejection, betrayal, loneliness and rejection. Love is unique and is only encountered when there is no fear, dependence or control. Never before that time.

***

Parable / Metaphor:

Long, long ago, God (however you understand it) came down to Earth and lived among the people, supporting and helping them in their daily lives. People flocked to Him in droves, asking for help and support, shouting over each other about who should be first, who has bigger problems and who should be heard first. God could hear nothing in the pandemonium, this hostile atmosphere. Wherever He appeared, the same thing happened, and He was tired of it. He wondered where on Earth He could find a place to rest for a while. He considered a very high and inaccessible mountain, but then concluded that in time people would reach Him there and the situation would happen once more. He thought about sheltering at the bottom of the ocean, but here too he came to the conclusion that human civilization was still developing and even in the depths He would not find a safe haven. Finally, he came up with a wonderful idea: "I will hide in their hearts, inside each one of them, they are sure not to find me there".

***

We should seek the source of our idea of what love is in our mother's womb, where we were safe in unconditional unity with another person. It was only later that we began to reciprocate our feelings. This is very deeply rooted in our subconscious. This pattern has become a deeply hidden dream of ours. This is how our mind was shaped. We have to be aware that no one, no matter whether he or she is our current partner or one dreamed up for the future, is obliged to provide us with love and happiness just because we expect it from him or her. The source of true love does not lie in meeting our needs or desires. Only when we look after our own development, when we have enough love within us to give and to share will we begin to attract people in a natural way, who will love us and become partners who create opportunities for us to grow and develop.

The word 'love' is frequently confused with the word 'desire'. Love is unconditional, not expecting anything in return. To love somebody means to allow them to be themself, to understand their feelings, concerns and worries. Love is selfless sharing with another person. To desire is to expect something in return. Desiring always expects to be reciprocated and is neither selfless nor unconditional. Desiring develops within your own body, but love in your consciousness. This means you can only give love to a deeply spiritual person. Sex is available to all. Familiarity is possible for all. Love is not. We often mistake the words 'I love' for the words 'I need'.

True love cannot contain even the tiniest grain of fear. True love demands courage, openness, sensitivity and above all, tuning into another's feelings. Few people understand and are aware of the difference between thinking about somebody and tuning into another's feelings. Thinking stems from the mind – the domain of thought. Often even when we think that we want the very best for somebody, we might generate a negative or even harmful perception, because we're all thinking in accordance with our own criteria, our own rules and our own judgments, and each person is different, unique. By being overprotective and overzealous, we will make the other person almost feel suffocated, without their own space or air. A lack of interest and care is also not the right attitude, but in excess they are bad, harmful and capable of destroying everything. Though our intentions may seem good to us, this does not necessarily mean that our actions are good. In this way, we unconsciously impinge on another's freedom, privacy or intimacy, and nobody likes this. Then that person's defense system is activated and the only reaction is "get away from me". This is what the mind focuses on, and not what we want to do or wish to communicate. Do not try to think for someone else. Love, but give freedom, more freedom. Everyone has their own life. Let them grow and go their own way, try not to interfere too much. What we can really do is love, always be very close and offer freedom.

Tuning into another's feelings comes from the heart, and the heart does not harm, impose, judge or compare. Such tuning-in leads to a deeper understanding of the other person and his or her behavior. The energy of two hearts is combined. Tuning into another's feelings is the highest form of love for another.

True love is a rare and beautiful flower that never blooms when watched over or controlled by the mind. It is important to rid yourself of the mind's fear and calculation. You cannot remain on your guard and in constant fear. You need to cast off your mask and armor, even when this would be highly risky and painful. This is the only way – taking the risk even when this comes with uncertainty and danger. Even when others might push you away or harm you. This is the still only way to be truly loved. The heart is always ready to risk and take up the challenge – the mind never.

> Don't use others to fill the void within you,
> calling it love.

When two people who do not love themselves meet, but dream of a great love, their world suddenly becomes beautiful. The beginnings of such a love are always beautiful, because nobody contaminates it with their destructive energy. The vision of fulfilling this dream erupts and a wonderful time ensues. Everything is wonderful, the mind writes a beautiful screenplay, creates an array of beautiful visions. At first, the two people pour all their positive energy out onto one another, for they believe that their partner will make their life wonderfully happy. Everything goes smoothly. Yet this beautiful time is soon over, as there is no inexhaustible source of love for oneself that can emanate outwards. After this 'honeymoon', when the energy that exploded with the dream of meeting one's "other half" being fulfilled, it appears that there is not enough energy to power two hearts, because neither possesses an inexhaustible source of love energy. They do not possess the seeds from which a beautiful flower can grow. They subconsciously count on the other person being the one to sow the seeds of eternal love, that they will be the source of happiness. Over time, positive energy runs out, because more often than not there is very little of it, while negative energy abounds. Once the honeymoon is over, the energy of love is in short supply and the subconscious, inner struggle begins as to who will manage this energy. Slowly and unnoticed, the gates of hell begin to open and it is difficult to comprehend what is happening; after all, everything had been so wonderful. It is difficult to understand what has happened. Such a beautiful relationship - why did it crash against the rocks?

It is very often the case that people whose hearts are lonely and in need of feelings easily fall prey to deceitful, false love.

Someone who doesn't love themself will never be able to love anyone else. The first flower of love must bloom in your heart. If it doesn't bloom there, it won't give you the seeds of love, and without these, you are unable to love another person. This flower must first bloom within you. This is the main reason why the great fire of love, which inflames the hearts of two people who do not love themselves, dies out so quickly. To be able to give love to the other person, you must first love yourself. You cannot share something that you do not have. You must have the seeds of love in you, otherwise every relationship will fall apart or remain a relationship mainly held together by the fear of loneliness or by force of habit.

Everyone knows that love is needed. They know that without love life is gray, devoid of depth and meaning, but few people can love. They do much in the name of love, but it is not true love. They confuse love with many other feelings, such as attachment, desire for possession and domination, addiction, jealousy, habit or fear of loneliness. All these feelings destroy the energy of true love. True love adds wings, gives freedom, creates opportunities for growth and development for both partners, there is no jealousy, fear of rejection or loneliness. It is closeness and compassion. It does not hurt, does not impose, does not limit, does not judge or compare. It is a profound understanding of the other person's inner needs, actions or behavior. If we want to change someone, it means that we don't really like them as they are. You cannot love and dislike at the same time.

Very often, when we become involved with someone, we see only what we want to see and conceal from ourselves what we do not wish to see. We unconsciously lie to ourselves simply to strengthen our conviction that this decision was the right one. As a matter of course, we assume that any imperfections will change under the influence of our love. This is certainly a crazy assumption. Our love won't change anyone. If someone is going to change, it's only because they themself want to do it. If this doesn't happen, we begin to notice what we didn't want to see before. What we were hiding from ourselves comes to the surface, out into the light of day. We feel hurt and disappointed just because someone hasn't adapted to our ideas and hasn't followed our script. We can't admit that what bothers us so much today has always been a trait of the person we willingly became involved with. All of a sudden, we start consciously trying to change the other person, and when this proves fruitless, our feelings of frustration and dissatisfaction grow. Of course, we put the blame for this on our partner; after all, we're the one with the perfect recipe for a great relationship, the most wonderful one in the world, but the only problem is that our partner does not want to change and adapt to our imagined version of events. They do not want to live according to what we see as our wonderful principles.

When you take the decision to spend your life with somebody, let them be the person you want to be with. Only get involved with somebody you don't wish to change. It's far easier than grabbing onto someone almost like a lifebelt, just to change them. The same goes in a situation where someone wants to share their life with you. They must love you as you are, not try to change you. Why tie yourself to one who doesn't accept you? After all, you know that a relationship like this will fall apart or die, devoid of feelings, spontaneity and closeness. You will be bound together solely by habit and the fear of loneliness.

True love accepts people the way they are without seeking to change them. To love somebody means to allow them to be who they are.

"If you love me as I am, that would be wonderful; I want to be with you. If you love me the way I am, OK, that's life, find somebody else who you accept the way they are". Such a way of communicating might seem overly direct, brutal even, but will certainly make our relations with others clear, unblemished, untainted by falsehood and hypocrisy.

The next significant source of relationship misunderstandings lies in our false assumptions that our partner knows full well what we're thinking and what we expect. We assume that they will do what we expect, but if this they don't act as we supposed, we feel disappointed or even offended. Most often, though, we use the phrase "you should have known". This attitude generally becomes the basis for pointless battles, stress and unpleasant situations. We ourselves are incapable of communicating what are often minor expectations to our partner in a clear and kind way. This leads to a crisis that poisons the relationship, but we blame our partner for their inability to read our mind. We construct a negative scenario in our minds, where our partner has not fulfilled our expectations because they don't love us, don't care, etc. More often that not, the other person has no idea what is going on, why we are dissatisfied, and yet we still do not try to clarify the situation, because our partner should know, shouldn't they? And so the downward spiral is set in motion, thanks to which what started out as a trifling matter blows up into the greatest drama.

The ability to discuss and express your thoughts, whatever they may be, without adopting a confrontational attitude or going on the defensive, will always have a healthy impact on relations and confirm the partners' maturity.

Jealousy is also becoming an extremely common cause of crisis or even of relationship breakdown. It is important to understand that it is an emotion, like many others. Depending on the importance we ascribe it and the energy we invest in it, it will affect our lives. If we endow it with a negative meaning, it will start to sap our energies, overwhelm and impair our capabilities, it will become a cause of frustration and discouragement. Never allow your life to be governed by such blind jealousy. It can ruin you and kill any love, even the very greatest. Such jealousy has nothing in common with love; it is merely a selfish desire to possess, dominate or limit someone else's freedom. If we endow it with a positive meaning, it will open up a wide range of creative possibilities. It will become our inspiration, propelling us forward, and becoming the driving force for wonderful goals and great plans. Depending on the energy we put into it, it will guide us towards a fall or rise.

***

The pace of modern life means that we have less and less time. We don't even notice what's happening around us. Everything in a hurry, without any depth. Everyone strives for something, desires something, wants to possess something, chases after something. Most things are done as a matter of course, routinely. We become so professional, efficient and effective in what we do that we are not fully aware of what we're doing. Everything becomes mechanical and automatic. Increasingly, we behave as if programmed, like robots, forget about ordinary human needs and feelings. We lose sight of intimacy, true love, the usual, everyday needs of families and loved ones. We have less and less time for the family, yet we increasingly allow ourselves shallow, meaningless meetings. Nowadays, the most common relationships are casual meetings, chit-chat, superficial acquaintances and occasional sex. The ability to forge close relationships is now lost. This is because we are afraid to expose our innermost, most vulnerable feelings. Opening up to another poses too great a risk to us; we might be hurt or mocked. Though on the surface, we are so strong and independent, in actual fact, deep down, we are sensitive, weak and lost. There is a certain risk in taking a chance on closeness with another, but without taking it, we will never know the love and closeness that we are so in need of. Hardly any of us can see that in this constant pursuit, this incessant rush, something has been taken away from us. We lose the ability to bond and are unable to love.

***

Love must be something real in your life, and not a kind of contract or dream. You must rid yourself of the mind's calculations, its anxieties and fears. It is never too late to experience true love for the first time. It will illuminate the darkness in the heart. Learn to love and your whole life will change. Take up this challenge with total commitment, belief and openness of heart, otherwise you will never see the beautiful reflection in the mirror.

Change your mindset and your life will change, too.

***

What you do today, what you think,
what you do in life, this is a step
that only you can take.
This step sets your course
for the future.

***

THE PATH

There are several thousand religions, sects and religious orders in the world and countless social circles or cultural centers. This means that we are dealing with thousands of different mindsets and various perceptions of reality that people around the world have. The circumstances we were born into, we were brought up and grew up in determine our perceptions of the world and our attitude towards it. These are also the conditions that shaped our ego, which lies at the heart of all conflicts, whether it is those taking place in the world around us or those taking place within us.

Because of the great diversity in ways of perceiving the world, and as a result, also in ways of thinking, any attempt at finding happiness and inner balance through changing the world or other people around us will never bring the expected results. Such efforts are doomed to failure. Because of the immense complexity of the reality surrounding us, there is no way of arriving at inner harmony and peace as long as you see them as being determined by the external circumstances. You can obviously build a wall enclosing yourself in your own comfort zone. Or you can live within the walls of your own dogmas and try to surround yourself only with those who think in exactly the same way as you, or act in line with your rules. But in this way you don't arrive at a solution; you only find a way to escape reality. It is just a way of incarcerating yourself in the prison of your own views, which will never provide you with complete peace or a sense of emotional security. It's because you can never be sure as to when, where and in what kind of circumstances an unexpected factor or a person will surface to disturb this fragile balance. The height of the wall is always directly proportional to the size of the threat. We are even incapable of estimating just how many reasons there are that may generate conflict between people, both of the external and internal kind. Therefore, there is no point in focusing on what differentiates the people around us nor in trying to find a solution to such differences.

The feature common to all people irrespective of their opinions, faith or material status is suffering. The broadly understood notion of suffering is determined by the mind's addiction to desire and resentment. Its meaning goes far beyond mere physical pain or misery. It also takes in all kinds of frustration, lack of satisfaction, grief, disappointment, aversion or despair. It is the result of our internal reaction to situations or circumstances that we are not ready to accept. Therefore there is no sensual pleasure that could shield us from it. There is no achievement or social status that could guard a person against suffering. Anything that is conditional is temporary. The only way for us to break free of suffering is to become independent of all kinds of conditioning.

Suffering is something very definable. It can be experienced and described. Suffering is not defined by some sort of myth, nor by supernatural and metaphysical concepts. This means that there must also be an understandable, simple and common path for all people to free themselves from suffering and achieve a state of inner peace and balance. This path is not based on any metaphysical methods or supernatural beliefs, but on acting in a particular, simple way. This way is understandable and logical, and requires neither intellectual knowledge nor the need to appeal to or entrust yourself to higher forces or a higher being.

> Your suffering comes not from the outside world but from your own mind, whenever external circumstances do not meet its expectations.

The most important thing is to identify the primary cause, the primary principle that triggers suffering. Only then will you be able to free yourself from it. An accurate diagnosis of the cause of the disease, which is common to all people in the world, can initiate an effective treatment process. One should not seek happiness as an antidote to suffering. Your peace of mind cannot be conditioned by external factors.

Only when you arrive at a deep understanding of the origins of all your suffering, which lies within you and means so more than just a blow from an external source, will you be able free yourself from it. You must have the courage to find within yourself the willingness to seek out a universal path that can free you from all negative circumstances. To understand this, you have to look really deep inside yourself and stop floating on the waves of self-admiration, sensual sensations and universally accepted norms.

Humans are the only beings on Earth that possess free will, which in turn is the root of their ego development. It is through ego that humans severed the bond with the Spiritual Energy of the Universe. They ceased to act in accordance with the laws of nature. This is the mythological, symbolic and metaphorical "expulsion from paradise". Everything that exists on Earth is subjected to the laws of the Spiritual Energy of the Universe. Everything is subject to the laws of nature.

Due to their possessing free will, humans are the only beings that have the possibility of living in contravention of these laws. By not following the laws of the Spiritual Energy of the Universe, we relinquish the natural security it provides and, at the same time, we attract everything that comes from negative sources of energy. Every person, with no exceptions, is born to be happy. Happiness is our inner nature. Children are happy, they laugh and play because they act in accordance with the laws of nature. They are open, trustful and deprived of inhibitions. As we grow up, we lose this capacity, due to the conditioning of the mind that is determined by the environment we live in. As we grow up and develop, we start to follow our desires and dislikes, which become the source of our suffering. Desires and dislikes stem from the conditioning of the mind. They were wired into our mind in childhood and later on in the process of our development. They are determined by the circumstances we grew up in, i.e. culture, religion, beliefs, the economic and political situation. However, it is not the external circumstances that determine our reactions but our mind's addiction to desires and dislikes, which stand for the opposite poles of our life. They are responsible for extreme mood swings depending on what kind of sensations we expect or experience at a particular moment.

If something is too heavy for you to bear,
stop carrying it.

Rid yourself of all feelings of guilt. Be aware of your mistakes and don't make them again, but do not blame yourself. Do not evaluate your past behavior through the prism of what you know now. Honest moral reckoning is enough, and this will help you improve yourself and also save you from generating excuses that might lead to improper and damaging behavior in the future. It is particularly important to make sure that this moral reckoning does not lead to feelings of guilt or injustice and therefore become the root of self-flagellation, which obviously has nothing to do with conscious and healing moral reckoning.

Nobody's perfect and everybody makes mistakes. To err is human. It is important to be aware of your mistakes and offer a heartfelt apology to those you have harmed, irrespective of their reaction or behavior. If possible, make amends or establish the way to rectify the situation and therefore not punish yourself any more.

By blaming yourself for your own mistakes, you make them grow within you and, consequently, you will never free yourself from them. What you start to hate is not so much your mistakes as yourself. In this way, you can change neither yourself nor anything in your life, as the rule goes: "whatever I occupy myself with will grow". In essence, in life we should avoid occupying ourselves with destruction. Overcome evil with good.

In order to understand this process better, let's imagine that you have 50 percent positive and 50 percent negative features of character. If you devote all your energy to nourishing and developing the positive features, they will grow and start pushing "the dark side" out. In this way, this 50 percent will grow into 60 percent, which will automatically make the negative features account for 40 percent, and so on. This simple pattern proves that a person who knows what they would like to change in themself, who is trying to combat their negative features of character, will never manage to change anything, because by devoting their attention to those features, they supply them with more energy, and in this way keep them alive, in line with the rule: "whatever I occupy myself with will grow". Obviously, in doing so you can develop some sort of system to control your behavior, but that's not the point here. You can't go on living under constant control, because then your life is deprived of joy and spontaneity. At the same time, all the negative features will explode with double the force at the point where you lose control. Therefore, we shouldn't occupy ourselves with destruction. It's better to spread good rather than struggle with evil.

You want to help somebody and give them a donation but don't really have time for them, so are you thinking about that person or yourself?

Beware of being good just for show. Be acutely aware of all your philanthropic, charitable actions. What is their true intention? Does such an activity grow out of a profound, selfless need of the heart, or is it just an unconscious trick of the mind to bring satisfaction, in the guise of charity, as compensation for all of their own negative actions, which we do not want to remember or from which we want to escape? True charity and concern for another brings no benefit whatsoever to the giver, not even a good sense of well-being. A good person is one who does good deeds without even thinking about them. You are a good person as long as you don't know it. As soon as someone starts to think about themself as a good person, or talks about it, then this has nothing to do with goodness. It is simply mental egotism, whose intention is only to improve one's own well-being. The other person becomes only a tool for improving self-esteem.

The ego says: "I'm a good person", "I'll gladly help you", "You should've said! I would have helped you", "I'm eager to help others". The heart says nothing; it just helps.

The quest for happiness, peace and inner balance is nothing more than the search for a lost childhood paradise. If we want to find our paradise on earth again, we must follow the path that will lead us to our goal. It becomes necessary to believe and know that the path we want to follow will lead us to complete and ultimate liberation from all suffering. This journey must be a lifelong relationship, not just an enjoyable, beautiful but fleeting romance. It must trigger inner perception that is stronger than just complacency. It cannot be merely a short-lived intellectual antidote to depression and doubt, or an escape to suppress dissatisfaction or problem.

Most of the anger and hostility we direct towards others stems from negative feelings we harbor about ourselves. As we develop and experience sincere, selfless love and goodness towards ourselves, the hard shell produced by self-destructive attitudes starts to dissolve, allowing love, goodness and kindness to flow to the outside. We start to develop selfless love for others as a form of sincere commitment to their well-being and happiness. It doesn't become the remedy for loneliness, nor will it constitute a response to moral demands or divine commands.

When you go to the shop, buy bread and flowers.
Bread to live and flowers to know how to live.

It is necessary to have a very deep understanding and strong convictions, and the awareness which goes with it that everything is subject to the laws of nature, and that every action, without exception, has its consequences. If we want to free ourselves from suffering, we must nip it in the bud, stop it at the point where it arises. If we don't find the root cause of suffering at its source, our work will have no value and no results. It's important to fully understand what the causes are and how they work. Any use of aesthetic medicine will defeat the object and will certainly not eradicate the source of the disease. The path must lead to a detailed analysis of the cause of suffering and, as a consequence, to a certain way of acting, rather than not just ending with the desire to free oneself from it. For this we need wisdom, which is not just a matter of learning and collecting facts. This wisdom must be cultivated in our daily lives. It cannot be an attempt to constantly seek pleasure as an antidote to suffering or to obsessively avoid unwanted situations. The blind pursuit of sensual pleasures as an attempt to quash dissatisfaction is short-lived and devoid of deeper value. This does not teach wisdom but makes us increasingly blind to our own weaknesses. Our mind becomes more and more obsessed with covetousness, aversion and delusions. Extreme renunciation of life's pleasures, escape into solitude or self-flagellation are not the right ways either. They do not lead to a happy life, in fact, they even mean surrendering and running away from it. The right path should heighten our awareness of the illusory nature of sensual lust and the futility of escaping from life or locking ourselves in the prison of our own comfort zone.

The primary source of suffering is the lack of awareness. It is here that all the other tendencies that induce suffering, such as conceit, vanity, covetousness, pride, jealousy, vindictiveness and arrogance have their origins. This is a lack of awareness of the far-reaching consequences of our intentions, thoughts and actions, and of the energy source from which they come. We can still search for sensual pleasures as an antidote to suffering, escape into pointless social encounters, put on the cloak of philanthropy and kindness, but this will not liberate us from suffering. To fully free ourselves from suffering, we must remove its roots, eliminate the unconscious from our lives. Remove the curtain of illusion and hypocrisy. Until we are honest with ourselves, not much will change in our lives. In order to achieve the ultimate goal of the path, which is to free ourselves from suffering, we must make our lives fully conscious. Unconsciousness must be completely eliminated. Stupidity must be replaced by wisdom. Practical wisdom develops slowly and begins with the consciousness of one's own misconceptions, behaviors and inclinations. Awareness of the invariably workable principle that all actions based on negative energy arising from such sources as anger, anger, desire for revenge, greed, shallow and vain desires to satisfy sensual needs will always have negative effects, while all actions coming from the depths of the heart, not at the expense of another person or nature, will always have positive effects.

As a consequence of the appropriate recognition and awareness of this process, moral discipline automatically improves, eliminating all subjective and biased assessments of our own behavior. Awareness of the energy source from which all our thoughts, intentions and actions stem helps us to develop an inner morality that is objective and unchangeable. This kind of life wisdom, understood not only as the accumulation of knowledge and facts but first and foremost as recognizing and suppressing the focal points of delusion, greed and aversion, we will enjoy liberation from all suffering. Such wisdom frees us from the conditions programmed into our mind, rendering it more open and objective. As a result, we begin to understand that there is no supernatural agent punishing or bestowing upon us temporal rewards and visions of happiness in some distant, celestial land, subjectively and at our own discretion. We become aware that everything that happens to us in life is a consequence of our intentions, thoughts and actions. We begin to live with the awareness that everything is an infinite ocean of energy, which, with all its power, endows us with the same energy that underlies not only our actions, but above all, our intentions and thoughts.

Humans do not stumble on the rocks
but on the tiny stones.

Our values, ideals, views and goals define our tastes, which in turn determine the thoughts and intentions that constitute the source of the energy sustaining us in life. They are the harbinger of our future actions. When misguided values and beliefs prevail, the result will be wrong intentions, resulting in wrong and harmful actions. Covetousness, aversion, revenge, jealousy or anger come to the surface in the form of thoughts that guide intentions. If our values are measured by the profit or social status gained, our morality will allow us to use all possible means to achieve the goal, regardless of the long-term consequences. This will lead to a situation where constant pursuit and rivalry become the norm, leading to incessant conflicts and obsessions, and consequently, to our own suffering.

Being unaware of the consequences causes us to flow with the current of greed and desire, seeking happiness in the blind pursuit of material worth. Shackled by greed and desire, the unconscious sees the way to happiness through them. Paradoxically, it is greed and desire that give rise to such feelings as disillusionment, unfulfillment or frustration. They also introduce into the unconscious a sense of threat or a fear of losing what we have already achieved or possessed. Unconsciously, we start to build a wall around ourselves to safeguard our achievements, our territory and our position. At the same time, this confines us to a prison filled with our treasures.

It is only being aware of the illusion of achieving happiness in this way that will eliminate such behavior from our unconsciousness. True happiness always has its roots in truth, and not in comfort. Initially, it encounters great resistance from the unconscious, which more often than not is anesthetized by the mirage of beauty. This mirage of beauty is indivisible from suffering. Suffering and greed are inseparable best friends - always together.

The two shortest answers – "Yes" and "No"
require the longest deliberation.

Transposing and reconstructing the burden of values is the only way to liberate ourselves from suffering. What is most important in the correct formation of values, views, ideals and goals is the awareness of their long-term consequences. We should consider whether we will not harm other people or nature along the way. True wisdom, which comes from an awareness of the principle that everything has its consequences, will shape our actions according to this principle. Awareness of this principle will automatically adjust our thoughts and intentions so that we act in accordance with the Spiritual Energy of the Universe. It will shape the thoughts that determine our intentions, which will lead to increased good will and not harming other people. Those actions of ours that cause harm to other beings deprive us of the right to be happy.

Covetousness, aversion, distaste, revenge, jealousy, hatred and rage are all deeply rooted in our minds. It is only an awareness of the consequences, the mirror image of laws, that can lead to them being uprooted. This results in suffering being banished. Thoughts and intentions rooted in true values, views, ideals and goals are sustained by the Spiritual Energy of the Universe, which leads to a lightness in their realization and will lead to a sense of fulfillment and happiness in future.

What can help in understanding this process is the conscious application of the following principle: I set the rules of the world that surrounds me. This principle may seem strange and incomprehensible, but let's look at it in greater depth – what it means and what comes out of it.

Every individual counts as one being and nobody counts as more than one. We are all equal by nature, in life and death. Nobody has more or fewer rights or privileges.

- If I start to lie, it becomes a rule. This means that everybody else, without exception, also has the right to lie to me. As a consequence, I have no right to bear a grudge against anyone else for behaving in accordance with the rule that I established.
- If I hurt someone or live at their expense, this means that I also allow everyone else, without any exceptions, to hurt me or live at my expense.
- If my source of income or the work I do directly or indirectly harms or is at the cost of others or nature, this means that I too consent to actions performed by others that might be directly or indirectly harmful to me.
- If the source of my livelihood brings suffering to others, this means that all others, without exception, may also engage in actions that will bring suffering into my life.
- If I deliberately exploit their lack of knowledge, or manipulate them to perpetuate this false conviction, this means that all others, without exception, have the right to treat me the same way.
- If I gossip, slander others and bear false witness, this means that all others, without exception, have the right to treat me the same way.
- If my behavior causes suffering to others, it means I too agree to future circumstances that will bring suffering into my own life.
- If I buffet and exploit others for my own benefit, it means that everyone else, without any exceptions, can do the same to me.

- If I buy any objects that were stolen, this means I also give all others, without exception, the right to steal from me, as this will also give them the right to buy at a bargain price.
- If I fail to keep the vows I voluntarily made, this means that all others, without exception, need not abide by the promises they willing made me.
- If I think negative and destructive thoughts, I generate a negative aura around myself, and as a consequence of the laws of physics and the principle of energy in the Universe, I will attract everything that is born of negative energy sources.
- If I evaluate and judge others, that means that everybody, without exception, has the similar right to evaluate and judge my life.

It's possible to come up with multiple examples, but the principle remains the same. The world that surrounds us is a mirror image of our intentions, thoughts and deeds. Life is simple. We are always sustained by the energy that underlies them. The examples above are not in the slightest intended as any kind of evaluation of anybody's actions. Their role is to open the consciousness to the universal principle of equilibrium in the Universe. Everybody has the right to act in the same way I do in whatever I do, and this should not lead to any dissatisfaction on my part, since I behave in exactly the same way.

Always act as if your deeds were bound by law.
Law that you yourself set is law
you respect and abide by.

We should always be aware of this principle, regardless of conditions or circumstances. We shouldn't use justifications such as "I did that because others do it". It is essential to take responsibility for yourself, without resorting to mind tricks that involve shedding responsibility and comparing ourselves with others.

Out of an understanding of this process and the awareness of its consequences grow correct thoughts and intentions, which thwart bad intentions while fostering moral actions.

Awareness of cause and effect means that the eye of wisdom opens up ever wider, freeing us from all suffering. True life wisdom is born of the consciousness of our own intentions, thoughts and actions. True wisdom uproots lust, ill will and the infliction of suffering. It annihilates any weeds that destroy even the best seeds. It gives rise to calm and mental balance. It provides the base on which true happiness can grow.

The path to ridding ourselves of suffering and to achieving a state of relaxation and inner balance should not be understood as a series of steps, one after another, in a predetermined sequence. Happiness, calm and life harmony are nothing but a rope made up of many separate strands. The reliability and durability of the rope depends on the number of strands. All these elements should be regarded as supporting and complementing each other, yet at the same time independent of each other.

The first basic strand, which in a way forms the core of the rope, will be a proper understanding of each situation, the sources of energy from which created it. What was the primary cause, the first spark that set the whole chain of events in motion. Proper understanding is the first step on the road. Without it, all the ones that follow will lead in the wrong direction, at most producing short-term complacency. Any journey without proper understanding will end in blind, chaotic steps, and being lost. To reach the goal, we must be completely sincere and honest with each other. This is the only way for us to discover the primary cause, whose source always lies within us. Only then can we cure it so that it can no longer infect our future.

You are the only one who can make yourself
happy or unhappy.

If we start to seek the causes outside ourselves, our mind will begin to come up with thousands of justifications and reasons independent of us, which will all lead us nowhere and bring none of the desired effects. If we try to set out in pursuit of external causes, and of shedding responsibility for our own life, the mind will enter such a train of thought and draw conclusions that will reinforce our convictions in something that is actually false. There is no factor in life more responsible for our unhealthy frame of mind and the suffering it brings than fallacious ideas stemming from incorrect understanding. Similarly, nothing can stimulate our creative powers more than an accurate assessment and correct understanding of the situation – the conscious and profound comprehension of the long-term consequences of our own thoughts. It entails understanding the energy source from which these thoughts flow, and as a result, which energy will sustain us in future. Will this be positive energy, giving us lightness and joy in our actions, or negative energy, which will mean everything is done with immense difficulty, at the cost of constant battles, sadness and dissatisfaction?

Pretended perfection, feigned kindness, being preoccupied with how others see us and what they say about us – these are a problem for huge numbers of people. This obsession makes us forget what truly is of the greatest value to us. Liberating ourselves from this obsession with ourselves and distancing ourselves from the needs of our ego gradually allows us to sense what really is most important to us in life.

True understanding is so much more than a simple evaluation done in accordance with the conditions of our own mind. This is an awareness of the source, the initial spark and the consequences of our own thoughts, intentions and actions. It is the consciousness of whether our behavior is objectively morally right, or fosters spiritual development, or whether its consequences will not prove harmful to ourselves and others.

Your future grows out of the seeds you sow today.

Do not let yourself be
enslaved by mediocrity.

***

No doubt you have seen a tree growing in an open space. It is so beautiful, it is so free. Nothing can to hinder its growth in all directions. Many people would find it a pleasure to sit under such a tree to take a rest and take in its good energy.

Would the same tree look as beautiful if it was growing in a forest?

Would other trees allow its unlimited development?

Does anybody notice a single tree in a forest? When you're in a forest, you only see the forest.

Would anybody notice a tree in a forest that is ill or has been chopped down?

Does anybody care about a single tree in a forest?

Do not live as if you were a tree in a forest; try to live like the tree which is free and whose development knows no bounds. Keep growing in all directions, blossom in the most beautiful way that only you can blossom, in the way that your heart desires.

You only have one life and this is your life.

***

EPILOGUE

It's high time we learned to put into words or actions what we are starting to understand and to embrace consciousness. It's high time we understood that the world around us is bigger, more beautiful and magnificent than the reality we see and are capable of interpreting through our five senses. It's high time we began to allow our hearts and intuition to guide us. The more we trust our intuition and have the courage to follow the voice of our heart, the more quickly we will detect the trickery and coldness so often hidden under a mask of friendship and politeness, or discover a wonderful, loving heart concealed beneath harshness and rage.

Guided by the energy emanating from the depths of your heart, it will be easier to achieve what you assumed was unattainable and to understand what you thought was incomprehensible. It will be easier to avoid those currents that bring chaos and start to swim with a current full of love and joy of life, achieving real happiness, gaining real strength and true friends. Living in harmony with the Spiritual Energy of the Universe, it's certain you won't have not to wait long for the positive.

There is no other path.

It's better to light a candle than curse the darkness.

***

Meditation is not related to any
religious system.

***

Appendix:

MEDITATE AND LIVE
AN ACTIVE LIFE

What is meditation and what benefits does it have ?

Changes in our external life are primarily due to scientific and technological development. The sources of this development are certainly to be found in the West. However, the sources of humans' inner development are mainly to be found in the East, where meditation has been common practice for thousands of years. The modern-day fascination with Eastern culture and its spiritual achievements also drives the increased interest in meditation as a path for personal development. Meditation has become the subject of serious scientific research and is an increasingly popular practice used in medicine and psychotherapy to arrive at the source of inner problems and cure them. Nevertheless, in Western culture, the culture of the mind and logical analysis, this is not yet commonplace and tends to generate the wrong associations. It seems to be something very solemn, as if only for those gloomy, serious people who have lost their joy and enjoyment of life. In silence they sit half a day in some strange and uncomfortable position. It has something of a monastery in it. Nothing more wrong. Although it must be admitted that more and more people in the West are beginning to meditate. Many very famous people who have been extremely successful on a global scale admit that meditation was the key to their success.

Several reasons why it is worth meditating.

- By meditating, you silence the constant stream of thoughts and at the same time achieve peace and mindfulness, which puts you in a state of maximum relaxation, improving your productivity. In this way, the effects of your actions are so much better and do not lead to stress.
- Meditation develops your creativity and creative thinking. It enhances your cognitive abilities and openness to the unknown.
- Meditation gives you energy, improves the memory and boosts our resistance to stress. It is the art of focusing attention and an antidote to the constant projections of the mind.
- Meditation is not an escape from life; the opposite is true – it is a huge step in the direction of life, a full life abounding in all its blessings, while at the same time maintaining inner peace and self-awareness.
- Meditation frees you life imprisoned in the fetters of your own thoughts, from the prison of your own mind, from a life filled with fear, anxieties, worries and irrational thoughts.

- Meditation fosters the development of self-awareness and positive emotions, improves health and leads to inner peace. It helps you discover the inexhaustible source of energy and strength, thanks to which we are able to move mountains.

- The essence of meditation is heightened mindfulness and awareness of both what is happening in your inner life and what is happening outside us.

- Meditation has a beneficial effect on our state of mind. It reduces feelings of anxiety and boosts serotonin levels in the brain. It leads to the spontaneous formation of new neural connections responsible for memory, learning, self-awareness, creation, and the regulation of emotions, stress and empathy.

Reject the old ideas about meditation. Don't believe that it merely involves sitting in some uncomfortable and incomprehensible position. The aim of meditation is self-improvement. It will open your eyes and make you more perceptive. Your heart will become more sensitive, conscious and loving. You will begin to see what you have not seen before. You will begin to delve into new spaces in your existence. Every moment of every day something new will happen. Meditation is like a bath that leaves you feeling fresh and purified.

Meditation can be compared to the light emanating from a bulb. It helps to illuminate the darkest corners of the human psyche, just as a light bulb helps to illuminate what is outside.

Most people believe that in order to achieve success in life, we need to struggle, concentrate fully, focus and fight. Yet this has many side effects. The more we struggle with something, concentrate only on it, and grapple with it, the greater the tension that arises within us, and the more tension, the weaker the effects. Meditation helps us to understand that in order to perform to the best of our abilities and give our all, we need maximum mindfulness and inner peace. However, to achieve this, we need to be in a state of maximum relaxation. The pressures of modern life make people experience anxiety and inner tension like never before. By meditating, we silence the constant stream of thoughts, at the same time achieving peace and mindfulness, which generates far better results. Only with peace and maximum mindfulness can we deal with something much greater. Our sixth sense, the sense of energy perception, is open, so we draw energy from the source of the Universe. This results in our actions being better and without stress or internal tension. One who truly meditates is joyful, embraces life, and is free of fear and anxiety. To experience joy they need no mood-improvers, such as alcohol or other stimulants. Joy flows straight from their heart. Meditation is a medicine for all sorrows, fears, anxieties and irritations.

In the East, psychotherapy has not developed as an effective aid in freeing ourselves from the deposits in our subconscious, because hardly anyone wants or is able to reveal their innermost secrets, the darkest side of their own behavior, in full. Neither psychotherapy nor psychoanalysis exists in the East. Meditation has developed there through the millennia. Meditation leaves you alone with yourself; you needn't tell anyone anything. You deliberately immerse yourself in the depths of your being, discovering your potential and freeing yourself from everything that lies concealed in your self's most hidden nooks and crannies. This allows you to liberate yourself from all the deposits in your subconscious, from the associated suffering. It heals your inner self.

The concept of meditation has been distorted in the West since the times of the Roman emperor Marcus Aurelius (2nd century A.D.), who wrote a book on the subject. In it he explains that meditation is a technique of deep concentration and contemplation. This is a highly distorted definition. Concentration and contemplation are activities of the mind. Meditation, on the other hand, is a state outside the mind. Its aim is to eliminate all thought projections flowing from the mind. Meditation is not a technique, but a process, a process of growing. Technique is always dead, and can therefore only be an addition. Processes are alive, evolving, developing. Meditation is growth, and this can not come about through technique, only through transformation, metamorphosis. And this can only be achieved through failure, frustration and error. You can't really learn about it from the outside, because no information coming from external sources will give you the essence of meditation. You might understand something, but any understanding derived from another person will remain something intellectual, and not from your own experience. Meditation comes to you from the depths of your inner self. Moving inwards, you notice how great a distance is created between you and the hustle and bustle that surrounds you. Just a moment ago you were almost at one with the noises surrounding you, yet now you are moving away from them. You begin to enter into a profound silence. As meditation deepens, you will feel the distance growing to the outside world.

Our mind is cluttered, even clogged up with old thoughts and memories. By meditating, we cleanse our mind of old rubbish, put it in order and create room for new ideas and sensations. When the mind is littered with thoughts and memories, it is very difficult to recognize good ideas and conceive of something new. When we meditate, we become more creative, we discern new ideas and ideas. Meditation is as essential to your mind as sleep is to your body. However, meditation should not be confused with concentration, as these are two completely different processes. During concentration, we mobilize our mind's various capabilities; during meditation, we avoid all mental activity.

Meditation is becoming an increasingly important element of an active life. More and more people in the West are beginning to learn the meditation of the East, just as more and more people in the East are learning the activeness of the West. In the modern world, meditation is becoming an indispensable element of active life, at the same time, in harmony with the voice of one's heart.

We often encounter the opinion that meditation is escapism, that it is only good for those who are tired of life. Such opinions are blindly churned out by people who have never had any contact with meditation, have never meditated and have no practical understanding of how great meditation is, nor of the benefits it brings in everyday life. These people are riddled with the fear of getting to know themselves and the great suffering they conceal within themselves.

Meditation is no escape; on the contrary, it is a form of great courage required for the journey deep into yourself. It is the courage to discover yourself and your hidden fears and anxieties. Only with such courage can you free yourself from these fears. It is the mind that is the main motivator of escape from oneself. It always finds a thousand reasons not to look deep inside yourself.

Meditation is the easiest path to seeing reality mindfully and consciously. It "unlearns" the mind from taking decisions too hastily, from making unreal, fanciful plans or assumptions. It creates a space between you and the surrounding world, giving time for a calm and balanced overview of reality, and thus helps make conscious decisions. Its essence is mindfulness and an awareness of what is happening both in your inner life and outside.

Do you feel that you're starting to lose control of your life, that you are often on edge, irritable and tired? When you put a stop to your anger, your rage, you produce a poison that spreads through your muscles and blood. Whatever you suppress within yourself affects your psyche and body, because they are linked to each other - they are a psychosomatic entity. Whatever happens in the body also happens in the mind, and vice versa. When you become irritated, toxins are released from the glands into the blood and the blood is poisoned. This is not philosophy, it is pure science. Every part of your body is filled with toxins, and in every muscle negative feelings are suppressed. During meditation, all these poisons are eliminated, and the internal flow improves. Using simple meditation techniques which can be practiced successfully at home, you will improve your mood, and gain more energy, vitality and joy of life. Meditation will help you to silence the constant stream of thoughts, thus bringing peace and relaxation. If you want to remain calm, mindful and aware of everyday life, start meditating.

Meditation is a refuge inside you. It is a temple where you can hide away. Whenever you feel tired, you feel that you have had enough, you can retreat there. Relax, wind down, restore your energies. But don't treat this as an escape from the world around you, as an escape from everyday problems. Meditation is a moment that will help you gain some distance; it will allow you to look at the same circumstances in a new, more conscious way. Meditation will bring many changes to your life, but remember that the biggest change does not involve discovering new lands, but looking at old ones afresh. Escape may bring you peace, but such peace does not provide the strength to face problems again. Meditation brings such peace and quiet into your inner self that despite the problems you encounter, this peace and quiet still remains.

There are two different kinds of peace and quiet: the first you cultivate, while the other appears on its own. Cultivated peace and quiet is nothing more than stifled hustle and bustle or an escape. This is not real peace, but is imposed by force and can explode at the slightest spark. It is peace that allows you to suppress any noise coming from outside, but you are still sitting on a volcano that can erupt at any time, any pretext will do. The peace and quiet that comes to you from meditation is something that emerges from inside you and is not forced. It first grows and builds up within before pouring out. This is a completely different phenomenon. It is catharsis and is a question of cultivating your own peace and quiet. True peace and quiet will only come to you through meditation. This silence will always be silence, it has a different dimension, a different taste, a different smell. It has its own beauty. Its depth is completely different.

The universe owes its entire development to cyclical changes, from elementary particles to whole galaxies. If we look around, we can see that there are cyclical changes occurring everywhere, which consequently lead to harmonious development. Humankind should follow nature by also making cyclical internal changes. The cyclical interweaving of activity and meditation is just as necessary as alternating work time with rest time. Meditation is the greatest rest for the mind. Start meditating without expecting anything. Any expectation is in vain, and is merely a by-product of the mind. A state not expecting and not evaluating is the greatest moment for transformation.

How to learn to meditate? The first steps.

True relaxation is a state where your energy stands still. Your thoughts do not wander to the past or future. This moment is everything, others do not exist. If you have a sense of time, you will not be able to relax. The clock simply has to stop, time has to stop. Energy remains in a state of motionlessness. Full relaxation is those moments when you don't need anything, and you don't want anything. This state is the greatest relaxation for mind and body alike. This state is called meditation. Meditation will provide you with the inner peace and quiet ordinarily prevented by the talkative mind, and enable your mind to rest. By allowing the mind to relax fully, literally turning it off, you will make it work more efficiently, more intelligently afterwards. Once you feel and understand what meditation is, it will accompany you everywhere.

Initially, this requires great self-discipline, so some come to the conclusion that it is very boring, difficult or hard work. This is a highly inappropriate and demotivating approach. It is definitely better to approach all such "novelties" as a challenge that can teach us something and offer new experiences. Every learning process is similar. It may seem boring or difficult at first, but as time goes by, we make progress and everything becomes easier. No one becomes a master on the first day. Take the first step towards improving your life.

Motivation is the key to everything we do. If we are motivated, everything comes easily. Ask yourself if you are satisfied with the incessant stream of different thoughts that "attack" you every day and cause uncontrolled mood changes that rob you of your inner peace. Meditation will first help you to calm down, and in time it will completely eliminate this inner turmoil. Repeat to yourself frequently: "I'm doing this to improve my mood, to gain more energy, vitality and joy of life. Everything I do, I do as best I can".

If you are a creative person with a very open way of looking at life and the world, it will be much easier for you to start meditating. On the other hand, if you are a withdrawn, fearful person unwilling to face new challenges or experiences and leading a very routine life, you may initially have difficulty meditating. This means that the mind exercises a lot of control over you. You find it harder to free yourself from it, so do something new every day, just a small thing, just to break out of your routine. Even small changes such as the way you talk, sit, talk to your loved ones, or schedule your normal daily activities will convince you that your mind is losing its control over you, that you are becoming a little more free. And this is the first big step to become a truly meditative person.

Meditation is a long journey and there are no shortcuts. This journey leads to an extremely profound transformation of consciousness. Becoming a truly meditative person is no easy task and won't be over in a flash. So don't expect too much right away and you will be less frustrated. Everything comes in its own time and at the right moment. Meditation is not an annual flower that blooms very quickly. Meditation is a plant that needs time to put down roots and grow to become a sturdy tree. Meditation is a great mystery, but don't rush to discover it. More often than not, hurrying causes delays. Meditation is only a success for those who are not goal-oriented. It is a state without thinking about goals, without expectations.

A lack of time is just an excuse.

Find a few minutes for yourself every day for calm meditation. If you are new to meditation, start with just a couple of minutes. When you have a moment, sit calmly and regulate your breathing. Loosen up, relieve the tension in your respiratory system. Forget about your problems for a moment. Transform the energy devoted to thinking into awareness and mindfulness. Close your eyes and focus on your breathing. Observe how you inhale and exhale. Don't force yourself to concentrate on this, because you will create a situation where everything disturbs you - every sound, every little noise. Meditation is not a matter of concentration. It is simply awareness. While meditating, we try to keep our mind "clean" and ensure that we don't think about anything. The aim is to soothe the emotions and calm the mind. Let your thoughts wander freely. Don't attach too much importance to them, let them flow. The mind naturally creates thoughts. Don't try to force them out. Relax and observe your breathing. Nothing else.

Start from a few minutes a day, then slowly extend the time. Initially, you may have difficulty sitting motionless and observing your own breath, even for such a short time, because it is not an activity you are used to. This may seem stupid or boring to you. With meditation, it is as with any kind of other training - if you repeat this activity for about three weeks, it will become a habit, giving you inner peace of mind, strengthening your mindfulness and self-awareness. You will see how calm your thoughts are, which will boost your motivation to explore the secrets of meditation.

Here is an example of a simple meditation technique. Sit comfortably with your back straight, on the floor or on a chair. Breathe through your nose, calmly and slowly, listening to your breath, paying special attention to exhaling fully. Concentrate on your body, relaxing every part of it and every organ in your mind. Breathing is the language of the body. When it becomes very even and calm, it means the body is relaxed. Then simply observe your breathing. It is helpful to observe your breathing in the area between your upper lip and nostrils. You will start to feel that the air you are breathing in is slightly cooler that which you are breathing out. Monitor these sensations without any emotion. When a stream of different thoughts starts to appear, ignore them, don't interact with them, don't judge them, but don't chase them away either. With time, all your old memories will start to rise to the surface. Do not give in to any emotions. Just remain an observer of these emotions. In time, they'll rise to the surface, disappear completely and cleanse you. Imagine that these are only clouds moving across the sky, and calmly return to observing your breath. Always let your breathing be your anchor. Each day, try to extend the exercise for a few minutes, but don't force it. Adapt your meditation time to your abilities. You will find that meditation will become something like a refreshing shower for the body and soul.

You can meditate everywhere. You can include meditation in your daily schedule, without having to sit in the lotus position. You can use your daily commute, standing in traffic, sitting on the train. Try not to think about anything. Watch your breathing as you draw the air in and let it out. Watch the thoughts that appear, without reacting. Do not judge them, do not interact with them, do not enter into an internal dialogue. Just watch them and calmly return to observing your breathing. Whenever you realize that you are thinking about something, go back to watching your breathing without any emotion. You can use any free moment you have for this. Sit down in the shower for a few minutes and meditate. In the morning, in the afternoon, take short a break four or five times a day to meditate, even for just five minutes. You will see that it will act like an injection of vitality. There is no need to meditate around the clock. Let it be simple, easy and light – in this way it will become as natural as possible. Don't force yourself to do it. Meditate when you have a free moment. Start meditating for a few minutes a day and gradually increase the time. Don't take it too seriously - treat it like fun. Don't turn it into a routine. With time, you will want to do it more and more often. Going deeper and deeper into your meditation, you will see how much space is created between you and the hustle and bustle that surrounds you. You will still be there all the time, it's just that the hustle and bustle will recede, and you will gradually liberate yourself from it. You will become an non-judgmental observer of what is happening around you. Your self-consciousness will grow with every moment. Meditation will become your safe haven within yourself, to which no one will have access. Your inner peace will have such power and strength that it will remain even in the face of the biggest problems or turmoil.

**

Meditation is nothing but finding a common
language with oneself. If you do not learn
to live in harmony with yourself, how do you
want to live in harmony with others?

**

ABOUT THE AUTHOR

For several years, I have traveled a lot. I have visited all seven continents and participated in expeditions to the highest mountains on each of them, as well as to the North and South Poles. While traveling, I meet ordinary people who are both immensely interesting and wonderful, and I learn about their culture, art, religion and everyday life. But above all, I learn about myself. Each person you meet is unique, one of a kind. Just like every human being, only getting to know yourself allows you to truly understand another person. I used to run a therapy center for young people addicted to drugs and alcohol. I paint and create installations. Sometimes I give old, forgotten and unnecessary objects a new sense of life – of life in art.

I have conducted meditations and therapies in various places in India and Nepal. I have managed an international team specializing in such things as internet marketing understood in the broad sense.

In the distant past, I was a 'Businessman of the Year', and an honorary consul.

A strong person who had no easy past behind him, I have experienced both spectacular successes and sensational failures in my life. Each time I bounced back stronger and kept moving. Today, I derive the greatest joy from small things, unnoticeable in everyday life, from contact with other people, and an appreciation of the little things that might seem insignificant to others but are of the highest value to me.

At some stage in my life I changed money into values, and expensive things into priceless things. I have found inner harmony and balance, and reconciled my heart with my head under the leadership of the heart.

Interests/Hobbies: Humans and their evolution; the history and development of art from its beginnings to contemporary art in correlation with the development of human consciousness; philosophers of the East and the West; mysticism; spiritualism; quantum physics; the Universe and its history; the development of civilization and human consciousness; energy and its transformation from the Big Bang to modern times; classical literature; opera; theater; paleontology; ...

***

To get to the top in life, you have to
go back a few times and
stop complaining
that it's uphill.

***

Printed in Great Britain
by Amazon